Ulrich Blum and Josef Schmid (Eds.)

Demographic Processes, Occupation and Technological Change

Symposium held at the University of Bamberg
from 17th to 18th November 1989

With 43 Figures

Physica-Verlag Heidelberg

Professor Dr. Ulrich Blum
Professor Dr. Josef Schmid
University of Bamberg
B.P. 1549
D-8600 Bamberg

ISBN 3-7908-0528-9 Physica-Verlag Heidelberg
ISBN 0-387-91398-X Springer-Verlag New York

Printing: Druckerei Schmidt u. Sohn GmbH, Mannheim 61
Bookbinding: T. Gansert GmbH, Weinheim-Sulzbach
7120/7130-543210

TABLE OF CONTENTS

INTRODUCTION

This conference was dedicated to the description, analysis and evaluation of demographic developments, especially to the long-term reduction in population size and the concomitant ageing of the labour force stemming from birth rates below the generational replacement level, in the countries of the European Community. Today, it is already predictable that these developments are bound to have repercussions on occupations and technological changes, although the recent developments in the East have partly postponed, partly reinforced these trends.

The drastic changes resulting from an ageing population have already been widely discussed with respect to the social security system, the maintaining of infrastructure, health services and the educational system, however, the direct and indirect effects on technological change and the resulting efforts to preserve one's economic position in the international competition have hardly been mentioned, thus far. In this context the Bamberg Symposium focussed on topics such as the question to what extent innovations depend on the social environment or the regional economic position, and how to adequately measure technological performance.

Prof. van de Kaa showed that there is a uniform tendency in the reduction of birth rates in Western and Northern Europe which is strongest in the Federal Republic of Germany and Italy, and leads to a reduction and ageing of these populations. Possible future development paths include the disengagement of individuals from family life, new competition from friendship networks, combinations of roles as the form and the rhythm of work changes due to technological change; tensions stemming from the necessity of adaption processes and different ways of burden sharing.

Even Greece can be regarded as an accelerated model of the trend described above. According to Prof. Dr. Tziafetas, Greece gradually falls in line with the other member states in respect to a rapid decline in fertility and a likely doubling of the share of old people, thus losing its traditional role as an emigration country.

Dr. Mammey stressed that migration is subject to the concentration of new technologies. Although companies are in most cases more mobile than labour, immigration into the European Community from the outside must be assumed, whereas no considerable migration within the countries of the European Community will occur in the coming decade.

Prof. Dr. Buttler demonstrated that the employment potential in Germany will fall in the Nineties; unification or immigration from Eastern countries will only postpone this. A policy to slow down the reduction of the employment potential will show only limited effects. The demographic wave that presently favours the labour market will slow down and fade totally in the Nineties; the mobilization of women for the labour market is a real opportunity because of their low participation rate in West Germany. However, an increase in female employment can already be seen, today. The last option, after having exhausted these possibilities, will be a technological and economic offensive in order to compensate for the declining and ageing employment potential, provided Europe, and especially the Federal Republic of Germany, want to maintain their social standards.

Prof. Dr. Lindley discussed the demand side of the future technological-industrial Europe. Today, we already find a recession in the demand for low-qualified labour in the industrial sector paralleled by a simultaneous rise in the demand for higher academic qualifications. The demand for labour will especially increase in the tertiary sector, with a specific stress on production-oriented applications. Even though the government holds an important position in tertiary activities, for instance in health services, and has contributed to an increase in employment, it can be reasonably assumed that it will - from a total perspective - hinder the development of the tertiarization of the society. Because of the interrelationship between employment, work contents and qualification, the problem of overqualification at the lower end of the employment spectrum exists especially for women. The increasing necessity to higher qualify the labour force causes pressure to externalize the costs; i.e., a possible rising vote of the public sector.

Prof. Wever and Dr. Wagenaar emphasized that in the short run the ability of an economy to innovate is more closely related to human capital than to accessible technologies. This links technological changes in an indirect way to the demographic component, as the transition from the educational sector to the employment sector will continuously slow down in volume, starting at the end of the Nineties. The integration of "blue- and white-collar" labour and the utilization of more than just one qualification (anti-Taylorism) will liberate considerable productivity reserves, and eventually overcompensate existing economies of scale. If in the development of enterprises other trends are accounted for, especially the decentralization of headquarters, the reduction in company slack, the sale of those divisions that are not directly related to the production of the very good and single sourcing versus global sourcing, a completely new spatial pattern for firm settlements may evolve. In the long run, differences among functions held by enterprises located in the center and those held by firms in the periphery will decrease. Attractive possibilities for new industrial locations, the acquisition of enterprises and the development of new firm organizations in the European Community will emerge. The distribution of the work force and its qualifications will have an increasing impact on those decisions in the future.

Problems related to the operationalization of the technological position of a country in respect to other countries were discussed by Dr. Koschatzky. From an analytical view, the relationship between demographic processes, the employment system and technological changes and innovations necessitates the definition and operationalization of the latter terms. However, the term innovation is often used in an ambiguous way. Innovations are not necessarily the result of an advanced techonolgical position of a country. Europe is an excellent example for having a brilliant technological position which did not lead to economic success. In this sense, the analysis of markets, especially the study of foreign trade data concerning technological intensive products, and the definition of the technological profile of a country, both shown in this paper, may partly solve the problem.

An unavoidable shortage in the work force is foreseeable. The rising potential of unskilled and low-qualified labour will ultimately give rise to a more costly formation of human capital. There are considerable doubts whether problems in production and employment can solely be overcome by migration processes. The increasing demand for higher qualified ("white- collar") employees will encourage non-European immigration into highly-qualified positions or into the tertiary sector. Within the EEC countries, migration movements of selected segments of the population are likely.

The ability to compensate for the ageing process and the decline in the work force by increasing labour participation is limited. The effect is twofold: on one hand, the transition of technologies from the educational system to enterprises and the public sector will become apparent. On the other hand - as a consequence - human capital will age and require additional investment to upgrade the eductaional system. Technological leadership is not a guarantee for economic excellence, in terms of the ability to innovate. The necessary societal environment may also be threatened by ageing processes.

As demographic processes and employment on one side and the economic and technological future on the other side are becoming increasingly interwoven, this conference in Bamberg had a pioneering character. We therefore thank the European Communities which sponsored this endeavour. We are indebted to Dipl.-Wirtschaftsing. Jan Siegmund and Ulrike Schäfer, MBA, who carefully prepared this volume. Thankyou to all participants who have enriched our kownledge on this topic.

Bamberg, July 1990

Ulrich C.H. Blum
Josef Schmid

OPENING ADDRESS

Peter M. Schmidhuber,
Member of the Commission of the European Community

Ladies and Gentleman,

In the course of the next day and half the papers which you will hear and the discussions which you will have will touch upon some of the major determinants of the economic and social fabric of Europe. The strength of the link between demographic trend and economic performance was perhaps most baldly stated by the British Prime Minister Sir Winston Churchill, when he commented that, "a nation can find no better investment than putting milk into babies". Without encroaching too far upon the territory to be covered by the impressive list of speakers, I should nonetheless like to offer by way of introduction some personal reflections.

Predictions of the United Nations suggest that in the course of the forty years from 1986 to 2025 the population of the present twelve member states of the European Community will decrease slightly from 324 million to 318 million. Over the same period the percentage of the population over 55 years old will increase from 13,4 % to 20,3 %. This ageing of the Community's population will profoundly influence the economic challenges with which we are confronted. It is clear that, ceteris paribus, it will result in a corresponding decrease in the percentage of the population which is economically active. The latter reduced percentage will have a consequently greater burden to carry in the form of pensions, health costs etc. Furthermore, this burden would become yet greater should there be an increase in the birth rate in Europe, thus adding further to the economically dependent part of the population.

In stark contrast to this the United Nations figures for the population of the world as a whole over the period 1985 to 2025 show an increase from 4.5 billion to 8.2 billion. Underlying these figures are dramatically high rates of population growth in the less developed countries and in the newly industrialized countries. These trends will lead to a completely different set of economic challenges, in particular to problems of unemployment and of training.

Such trends on their own may be expected to lead to a widening of the gap in income per capita between the developed world and the less developed world.

Technological progress can contribute to the widening of this gap by reducing the general labour constraint to further economic development in the industrialized world. However, this does not rule out the possibility of specific shortages resulting from the requirements for ever more skilled labour to work with new technologies. The future shape of the world economy will be decisively influenced by the succes of the industrialized world in achieving higher productivity through the development of new technologies compared with the success of the developing world in achieving economic growth by the adoption of existing technologies.

It is clear that at both Community and world level the resolution of the problems resulting from demographic trends and technical changes will be one of the major challenges of the 21st century. I therefore wish the present symposium, dealing as it does with such important themes, every success.

"THE GREAT DIVIDE"; ON DEMOGRAPHIC TRENDS IN THE EEC

Dirk J. van de Kaa
Netherlands Institute for Advanced Study in
the Humanities and Social Sciences

0.   "THE GREAT DIVIDE"

The mid-sixties appear to form a watershed, a "Great Divide", in the demographic history of the twelve countries which now constitute the European Community. They divide that history in what one may concisely call an "altruistic" and an "individualistic" period (van de Kaa, 1987). These two terms have the merit of being remembered fairly easily and of indicating certain features of the pre-1965 and post-1965 periods quite well, but they obviously lack in refinement, sophistication and in capacity to describe the complex reality in a series of countries. Nevertheless, it is instructive to conceive the mid-sixties as a "Great Divide", marking very significant shifts in fertility and family formation, mortality and international migration which have altered the demographic prospects of the Europe of the Twelve, fundamentally. The two periods can be contrasted best by naming the six demographic shifts, which will dominate Europe's demographic future:

1.   From the golden age of marriage to the dawn of cohabitation;
2.   From the era of the king-child with parents to that of the king-pair with a child;
3.   From preventive contraception to self-fulfilling conception;
4.   From the uniform to the pluriform household and family;
5.   From social to biological longevity;
6.   From emigration to immigration.

In the following paragraphs these shifts will be sketched in broad terms using mainly period measures. Their implications for the future will be highlighted by relying on UN-projections published in 1989.

1. TRENDS

1.1 Fertility and Family Formation

One of the most striking shifts in the demographic behaviour of the European population occurred in the marriage pattern. From the mid-sixties, when marriage was quasi-universal, a very rapid decline in total first marriage rates took place. Table 1 illustrates this decline in some detail and suggests that, if current levels were to continue, only 50 to 70 % of all women would ever conclude a first marriage; the picture for males being only marginally different. Such figures are, however, likely to be misleading in that concomitant with the decline, more complex phenomena can be observed. The mean age of women at first marriage, for example, tends to show a U-shaped curve over time, with mean ages decreasing during the late sixties and early seventies and increasing thereafter (Hoffmann-Nowotny; Fux, 1990). Thus, period effects are certainly important and in some cases marriage may simply have been postponed. It is, further, evident that the countries of the Twelve are not homogeneous in regard to their marriage pattern and neither are the populations within individual countries. Considerable differences in lifestyle and accepted behaviour exist. Moreover, as the most recent figures for Sweden demonstrate (The number of marriages to women resident in Sweden rose to 108.765 in 1989 compared with not more than 40.000 in each of the years 1970-1988, as a result of a change in social security entitlements. (Hoem, p.c.)), marriage may become very susceptible to policy changes and may, consequently, already have lost some of its power as an indicator of public mores and relational intentions. It is important to note in this context that the U-shaped curve of change in the age at first marriage followed rather than preceded changes in fertility behaviour. It was the availability of good, modern contraception which first allowed people to marry young and yet not have children for some time, thus generating the decline in age at first marriage. In turn, this pattern of early marriage with delayed childbearing made the "paperless marriage" or cohabitation an acceptable option, thus generating the increase in age at first marriage and the reduction in total first marriage rates.

That the "Golden age" of marriage has passed is also evident from the increase in divorces and the continually increasing fractions in the population which prefer cohabitation to marriage. In several of the EEC-countries (Denmark, U.K., France, F.R. Germany, Netherlands) the total divorce rate currently exceeds 30 per 100 marriages. This suggests that in those countries in the order of a third of all marriages are likely to end in divorce, while divorce will on average occur at a shorter duration of the marriage. And, while in other countries divorces may still be relatively uncommon, the prevailing tendency usually is upward.

Cohabitation in consensual unions escapes routine registration of vital events. Knowledge about this phenomenon is derived mainly from sample surveys. Table 2 presents a picture for the EEC-countries for which data has been collected. Where a time perspective exists, the increase in cohabitation is very marked in all age groups, although at each date cohabitation tends to be more popular amongst the young. The changes in the total proportions of each age group in union tend to be more limited. Of the women aged 30-34 almost invariably between 80 and 90% live together with a man in a more or less stable relationship.

The speed of demographic change in the EEC-region and the simultaneity of the changes in the region has never been more apparent than in the decline of the total fertility rate. Table 3 shows the value of that index in 1950, 1960 and 1988, or the most recent date available, while figures 3 a, b and c graphically depict the rapidity of the observed changes between 1965 and the mid-eighties. Figure 1, finally, gives a picture of the most recent geographic pattern. The material presented makes clear that the twelve countries concerned, appear to follow a similar transition, albeit with slight differences in timing; Northern and Western European countries precede those of the South. With the exception of Ireland current levels fall well below those needed for the long-term replacement of generations, with the figures for the UK and France being noticeably higher than elsewhere. A more detailed analysis of recent years reveals that the pace of decline is slackening and that a low plateau has been reached, but also that changes in tempo continue. There is clear evidence of a continued increase in the mean age of childbearing in those countries for which such data is available (Szabò, 1988:19) and more generally, of an increase in age specific fertility rates at higher ages of the mother. During the decades when the total fertility rate dropped sharply, the proportion of children born out of wedlock amongst all births rose. Table 4 contains evidence of this phenomenon, which is universal and seemingly independent of the original level. The range of values found is, however, in many respects amazing, especially in countries that are tied together by such strong economic bonds. Differences in cultural heritage seem to be quite important in this respect, and this partly explains why the illegitimate birth rates in Southern Europe tend to be lower than elsewhere.

The changes in fertility patterns just observed are indicative of the change in emphasis in the lives of people before and after the mid-sixties. In the pre-1965 period marriage and the family were of central importance. Parents limited the size of their families to the numbers they could provide for with a proper education, and concentrated their attention on those children. They practised family planning for "altruistic" reasons, in the sense that concern for the welfare of their family and their offspring constituted the main motivation. The child was "King". After 1965 "individualistic" motivations begin to dominate. Aided and to some extent generated by the advent of modern contraceptive techniques and methods, individual rights to self-fulfillment increasingly determine the choice between marriage and cohabitation, between the continuation of a stable relationship and a separation, and between the choice for or against children. Children are valued, but largely for the way in which they enrich the life of the pair. The emotional satisfactions of parenthood are achieved in the most economical way possible by having one or perhaps two children.

Contraception is practised permanently using the pill, the IUD and, if no further children are desired, by sterilization of one of the partners. Contraception is only interrupted, once a deliberate choice for having a child is made; this positive choice no longer depends almost exclusively on one's marital status or the permanency of a relationship. Self-fulfilling conception replaces preventive contraception.

There is a great deal of fairly scattered evidence that the trends in fertility and marriage/divorce patterns, just described, have had a profound impact on the formation and composition of households and families. In addition, young people have tended to leave home earlier than before, the number of "others" (servants, relatives) in the households has declined, and the sex differentials in life expectancy have increased, with the consequence that the average household size is now much smaller than two decades ago (Schwarz, 1988).

A recent overview of available information presented by Keilman (1988), suggests that in the EEC the proportion of households which comprise of a couple with children only, declined more between 1960 and 1970, than after that date.

What would seem to be the most significant development from a conceptual point of view, is the apparent propensity of people to live alone, and for people to accept the single parent status with a certain ease. Between 1960 and 1980 all European countries for which data was available, showed an increase in the proportions of one-person households. "Current" levels show values of between 20 and 30% in Northern and

Western European countries and values between 10 and 20% elsewhere (Keilman, 1988: 313). The proportions at younger ages (say, below age 35) have usually increased more rapidly than those at higher ages. This partly demonstrates the effect of children leaving their parental home earlier than before (Kiernan, 1986).

A number of fairly recent papers allow the compilation of a table (Table 5) showing the distribution of one-parent families by marital status and sex in 4 countries. Although, the absolute figures are small, it is evident that those singles are predominantly women, while amongst men separation and widowhood tend to be rather important causes of being a single parent. In the case of divorce, women seem to remain responsible for the children more frequently than men.

The rapid growth of one-person households is indicative of a development in which "living alone" is no longer a question of "force majeure" but it is, at least to some extent, a voluntary decision. This is individualism at its limits.

1.2   Mortality

Figure 2, which shows the life expectancy of women at birth in European countries, clearly shows that the greatest contrasts in mortality occur between the countries of East Europe and the rest. While in Eastern Europe social factors, such as excessive drinking, eating fat-laden diets, poor housing conditions etc., still determine longevity to a considerable degree, in the EEC-region life expectancy is pushed towards its biological limits. Appropriate life styles and good medical care have improved the survival chances, particularly at the somewhat higher ages. For women, a life expectancy at birth of 80 years or more has been realized in quite a few countries. For men the gains have been somewhat less impressive so that the difference in life expectancy at birth between men and women is larger than before and is frequently in excess of 5 or 6 years.

1.3   International Migration

From a region which for many decades has sent people to other continents, Europe has become a region of immigration. Immigrants began arriving in the EEC-countries in the early to mid-sixties. The early influxes subsided with the recession of 1967 but mounted again until in 1973 the oil prices quadrupled, and a recession began. The major migration streams began as planned recruitment of guestworkers. Currently unplanned streams prevail. They result from family reunification, refugees seeking political asylum, entry permits given for other humanitarian reasons, and free movements within the region. For most EEC-countries the period of 1980-85 was one of net-immigration (Table 6). Recent events in Eastern Europe have had a fairly profound influence on flows to the F.R. of Germany and may, in future, well affect other countries of the Twelve. Future flows will, without doubt, also be influenced greatly by the way in which the EEC reacts to migratory pressures from the Northern Mediterranean and other Third World countries.

2.   PROSPECTS

The changes in population trends just described have altered the demographic prospects of the EEC-region quite significantly. Although, in 1987 the excess of births over deaths still amounted to about 620 thousand per year, and thus was still higher than the growth resulting from net migration (412 thousand), the time may not be far off that this constellation will be quite different. For the rate of natural growth has already substantially and continuously declined since the mid-sixties, while since 1982 the influx of migrants appears to be mounting again (Table 7). What the precise course of events is likely to be is almost impossible to predict.

2.1   Mortality

That the increase in life expectancy for males and females will continue is fairly certain. Hämäläinen (1988) who studied the mortality assumptions underlying national population projections in European countries found predictions as high as 83.5 years for women and 76.0 years for men (see Table 8). Usually only one assumption in this regard was used for all variant projections, and this is understandable, given the limited influence small variations in life expectancy have on the development of the population size.

2.2   International Migration

Movements in international migration are so volatile and subject to policy measures or economic changes, that people preparing national or international projections, in many instances, refrain from formulating specific assumptions about them. Frequently, an official policy statement that a country does not consider itself to be a country of immigration, or an official policy objective to have zero net migration, is sufficient reason not to take international migration into account as a potentially important element of population growth. Table 9, compiled by van der Erf (1988), demonstrates that, in national projections at least, the expectations regarding future migration trends are quite varied. There is little doubt, that the size and origin of future streams will to a large extent be determined by such policies as the Commission will develop in the context of, or following the 1992 Single Act. Currently, foreigners originating from countries other than EEC member states, form only a small fraction of the population in the region (Table 10). Good arguments can be advanced for the thesis that this fraction will gradually grow, and that the EEC will continue to show a positive rate of net immigration for decades to come (van de Kaa, 1989).

2.3 Fertility

Decisive for future population growth in the Europe of the Twelve is the fertility behaviour of its population. Several scenarios are conceivable in this regard. One could possibly assume a continued drift in the direction of greater individualism and, consequently, of a further decline in the willingness of people to commit themselves to stable unions and the responsibilities of parenthood. An alternative would be to consider the possibility of disenchantment setting in, with the consequence that new cohorts entering the reproductive years may act quite differently from their parental generation. A third scenario would be to assume that governmental intervention will change current trends. This, partly by adjusting societal conditions in such a way that combining parenthood with other options (career, employment) becomes an attractive alternative, and partly through tax adjustments or adjustments in the social security system which would make divorce, childlessness, or having a very small family only, less attractive.

Although the most recent trends make a slight increase in fertility somewhat more likely than a further decline, there is very little evidence that would suggest a rapid return to levels at or well above the replacement level. In a few countries, the complete family size of women born around 1950 may come close to that level, but this is not a general phenomenon. In national population projections a continuation of low fertility levels is usually the most likely variant but, as Table 11 shows, a return to replacement level fertility is also a favoured assumption. For their 1988 medium variant, the United Nations assumed a modest rise in virtually all EEC-countries (Figures 3a, b and c).

2.4 Projection results

Results of population projections for EEC member states, or at least part thereof, have been published by a variety of researchers and organizations (Macura; Malajic (1987), World Bank (1988), Eurostat (1988)). The most recent figures, arrived at by the UN (1989), result in the medium variant of a modest decline for the EEC-region as a whole between 2000 and 2025 (329.830 million versus 325.615 million). These figures do not, of course, anticipate German reunification, and neither do they incorporate net migration. Of particular interest in these projections is the decline in the proportion of women of fertile ages in the population that will occur as a result of the decline in birth rates since the mid-sixties and the fertility assumptions illustrated in Figure 3. This proportion (see Figures 4a, b and c) declines steadily from about 1990 onwards, albeit with some variation in date and speed from country to country. From peak values of 25 to 27% around the early- or mid-nineties, these fractions tend to drop to 19 to 21. Notwithstanding the slight rise in total fertility rates assumed, this results in relatively flat curves for the numbers of births expected to be born in the EEC-countries concerned (Figures 5a, b and c). The number of children expected to be born in the beginning of the next century invariably fall below those of the mid-eighties and greatly below those of 1965.

The age structural effects of past trends together with those assumed for the future are very marked, indeed. The proportion of young adults in society (people aged 15-24) will, again with certain differences in timing, fall from about 15 to 17% around 1985 to figures in the order of 11 to 13% by 2005. One may safely predict that such a scenario materializes pressures to allow a substantial inflow of migrants to occur. But then, predicting demographic trends for more than a few years ahead has always been a thankless exercise, and one may safely assume that the time of surprises has not passed, yet.

ACKNOWLEDGMENT

The author wishes to thank Drs. Yves de Roo of NIAS for preparing the illustrations.

REFERENCES

Blanc, O. (1985), *Les ménages en Suisse. Quelques aspects de leurévolution de 1960 à 1980 à travers les statistiques de recensement,* in: Population 40, no. 4-5, pp. 657-674.

Callovi, G. (1988), *The Prospects for International Migratory Flows within the European Community at the Approach of the Third Millennium,* paper presented at the International Seminar on the Ageing of Population, Futuribles International, Paris, 4-5 October 1988, 25 pp.

Clason, C.E. (1986), *One-parent families in the Netherlands,* in: Deven, F. and Cliquet, R.L. (eds.), One parent families in Europe, a NIDI/CBGS publication, The Hague, Brussels, 1986, pp. 195-209.

Council of Europe (1989), *Recent Demographic Developments,* Strasbourg,1990.

Van der Erf, R. (1988), *External Migration Projections,* paper presented at the International Workshop on National Population Projections in Industrialized Countries, Voorburg, October 1988.

Eurostat (1989), *Demographic Statistics,* Luxembourg, 1989.

Hämäläinen, H. (1988), *Comparison of Projected National Mortality Trends in Industrialized Countries,* International Workshop on National Population Projections in Industrialized Countries, Voorburg, October1988.

Hoem, J., Private communication, 1990.

Hoffmann–Nowotny, H.J. and Fux, B., *Present Demographic Trends in Europe,* Zürich, 1990, (Ms), 26 pp.

Van de Kaa, D.J. (1987), *Europe's Second Demographic Transition,* Population Bulletin, Vol. 42, No. 1, March 1987, Washington: the Population Reference Bureau, Inc., 1987.

Van de Kaa, D.J., *The Second Demographic Transition Revisited: Theories and Expectations,* Paper presented to the Conference on Population and European Society, Florence, 7-9 December 1988.

Van de Kaa, D.J., *Europa 1992 en het vraagstuk van de internationale migratie (Europe 1992 and the question of international migration),* in: Het open Europa en de ruimtelijke ordening, Delftsche Uitgevers Maatschappij, 1989, pp. 49-63.

Keilman, N. (1988), *Recent trends in family and household composition in Europe,* European Journal of Population, Vol. 3, 1988, pp. 297-325.

Kiernan, K.E. (1986), *Transitions in Young Adulthood,* paper presented at the Conference on Population Research in Britain, British Society of Population Studies, Norwich, September 10 – 12, 1986.

Macura, M.; Malacic, J., (1987), *Population Prospects for Europe,* in: Plenaries, European Population Conference, Jyväskylä, 1987, pp. 1-45.

Mennitti, A.; Palomba, R. (1986), *Some aspects of Italian one-parent families,* in: Deven, F. and Cliquet, R.L. (eds), One Parent families in Europe, a NIDI/CBGS publication, The Hague, Brussels, 1986, pp. 173-195.

Moors, H.; van Nimwegen, N., *Social and demographic effects of changing household structures on children and young people,* NIDI, The Hague, 1990, (Ms), 31 pp.

Monnier, A. (1989), *La conjoncture démographique, l'Europe et les pays développés d'outre mer,* Population (44), 4-5, July/October 1989, pp. 901-923.

Schwarz, K. (1986), *One-parent families in the Federal Republic of Germany,* in: Deven, F. and Cliquet, R.L. (eds.), One Parent Families in Europe, a NIDI/CBGS publication, The Hague, Brussels, 1986, pp. 141-154.

Schwarz, K. (1988), *Household trends in Europe after World War II,* in: N.Keilman, A. Kuijsten, and A. Vossen, (eds.), Modelling Household Formation and Dissolution, Oxford: Oxford University Press, 1988, pp. 67-83.

Szabò, K. (1988), *Comparison of Projected National Fertility Trends,* International Workshop on National Population Projections in Industrialized Countries, Voorburg, October 1988.

United Nations (1989), *World Population Prospects, Estimates and Projections as Assessed in 1988,* Population Studies, no. 106, New York,1989.

World Bank, *World Development Report,* Published for the World Bank, Oxford University Press, various years.

TABLES AND FIGURES

Country	Year	1965	1975	1986
Denmark		984	661	&572
Northern Ireland		952	942	690
England & Wales		1002	876	&665
Scotland		1023	889	696
Belgium		1002	888	660
France		993	858	&524
Fed.Rep.Germany		1102	764	@598
Luxembourg		--	799	@666
Netherlands		1130	827	&601
Greece		1185	1158	*875
Italy		1024	931	700
Portugal		1012	1275	790
Spain		982	1024	#690

* 1980; # 1984; @ 1985; & 1987

Sources: van de Kaa, 1988; Monnier, 1989

TABLE 1:   Total First Marriage Rates in Selected E.E.C. Countries, (Females), 1965-1968

Country	Age Group	20-24	25-29	30-34
Denmark	1975	44.6	11.9	5.7
	1981	65.2	29.4	13.5
United Kingdom	1976	3.4	3.6	2.3
	1980	11.1	6.2	2.3
Belgium	1985	*23.8	----- 7.7 -----	
France	1975	5.9	2.5	1.1
	1980/81	16.3	6.4	2.4
	1986	35.8	14.0	10.1
Fed.Rep.Germany	1985	-----	#11.2	-----
	1988	-----	#13.4	-----
Netherlands	1980/81	28.0	13.0	5.0
	1982	31.4	11.1	4.6
	1985	36.3	15.9	6.7
	1988	46.3	21.3	8.4
Italy	1983	2.4	1.6	1.8

* 15-24; # 18-35

Sources: Van de Kaa, 1988; Moors and van Nimwegen, 1990

TABLE 2:   Consensual Unions as a Percentage of All Unions in Selected EEC-Countries, by Age of the Woman, Specified Years

Country	Year	1950	1960	1988
Denmark		2.58	2.54	#1.50
Ireland		--	3.75	2.17
United Kingdom		2.22	2.69	1.83
Belgium		2.34	2.52	1.56
France		2.93	2.73	1.82
Fed.Rep.Germany		2.10	2.37	1.40
Luxembourg		--	2.29	#1.41
Netherlands		3.09	3.12	1.54
Greece		2.57	2.23	*1.62
Italy		2.49	2.41	1.33
Portugal		3.04	3.13	#1.56
Spain		2.46	2.79	*1.53

* 1986; # 1987

Sources: van de Kaa, 1988; Monnier 1989; Eurostat 1989; Council of Europe 1989

TABLE 3: Total Fertility Rates in EEc-Countries, 1950-1988

Country	Year	1965	1975	1986
Denmark		9.5	21.7	#44.5
Ireland		2.2	3.7	9.6
United Kingdom		-	9.0	21.0
Belgium		2.4	3.1	* 6.3
France		5.9	8.5	21.9
Fed.Rep.Germany		4.7	6.1	9.6
Luxembourg		3.7	4.2	10.2
Netherlands		1.8	2.2	8.8
Greece		1.1	1.3	1.8
Italy		2.0	2.6	# 5.8
Portugal		8.3	7.2	12.8
Spain		1.7	2.0	5.2

TABLE 4: Illegitimate Births as a Percentage of Total Births in the EEC-Countries, 1965-1986

Country	Year	Single		Separated		Widowed		Divorced		Total	
		m	f	m	f	m	f	m	f	m	f
Fed.Rep.Germany	1982	--	11	22	10	50	47	28	32	257*	1388*
Netherlands	1983	10	13	--	6	41	21	48	60	---	----
Switzerland	1980	--	7	17	12	57	46	26	36	15	94
Italy	1983	--	4	15	17	83	75	2	3	166	965

Marital status

* One parent families with single children and single children and other persons living in the household.

Sources: Blanc (1985); Schwarz (1986); Menniti and Palomba (1986); Clason (1986).

TABLE 5:   One Parent Families by Marital Status ans Sex of Parent, in Selected European Countries, around 1980

Country	Year	Net immigration
Denmark	80/86	0.7
United Kingdom	80/86	- 0.1
Belgium	80/84	- 1.2
France	80/84	0.6
Fed.Rep.Germany	80/84	0.4
Netherlands	80/86	1.4

Source: Van der Erf (1988)

TABLE 6:   Net Immigration in Selected European Countries (Annual average per 1,000 of the 1985 midyear population)

Year	Population size per 1-1- (x 1000)	Natural growth over:	Migration over:	Birth rate	Death rate	Natural growth rate	Rate of net migration
				Per 1000 average population			
1965	292 007	2422	- 35	18.7	10.6	8.2	- 0.1
1970	302 354	1766	92	16.4	10.6	5.8	0.3
1975	311 276	991	305	13.8	10.7	3.2	1.0
1980	317 110	876	654	13.0	10.3	2.8	2.1
1987	323 264	620	412	11.8	9.9	1.9	1.3

Source: Eurostat 1989

TABLE 7:   Total Population, Natural Growth, Net-Migration and Vital Rates, EEC, 1965-1987

Country	Male life expectance at birth			Female life expectance at birth			
	2000	Highest value	Year of highest value	2000	Highest value	Year of highest value	Number of assumptions
Denmark	71.6	71.6	1985	79.0	79.0	1995	1
Ireland	71.2	72.3	2021	77.1	78.5	2021	1
Un.Kingdom	74.0	75.1	2050	79.4	80.2	2050	3
Belgium	73.3	73.3	2000	79.5	79.5	2000	1
France[a]	73.1	74.0	2020	81.5	82.4	2020	2
F.R.Germany	73.4	73.4	1995	79.8	79.8	1995	1
Luxembourg	72.8	74.1	2050	79.4	80.7	2050	1
Netherlands	74.5	74.5	2000	80.5	80.5	2000	3
Greece	73.9	73.9	2000	79.6	79.6	2000	1
Italy	75.0	76.0	2020	82.1	83.5	2020	1
Portugal	70.2	70.2	1985	77.1	77.1	1985	1
Spain	72.5	72.5	1980	78.6	78.6	1980	1

[a] 'basse'

Source: Hämäläinen (1988)

TABLE 8:   Life Expectance at Birth by Sex, in Selected EEC-Countries, 2000, Highest Value and Year of Highest Value, (national projections)

Country	Period	Net immigration per 1,000
Denmark	90/99	0.4
	00/20	0.0
Ireland	90/00	- 1.3
	01/20	- 0.6
United Kingdom	90/99	- 0.3
	00/50	- 0.3
Belgium	90/99	- 2.3
	00/20	- 2.1
France	90/99	0.0
	00/20	0.0
Fed.Rep.Germany	90/99	0.4
	00/29	0.2
Netherlands	90/99	1.9
	00/20	1.9

Source: Van der Erf (1988)

TABLE 9:   Projected Net Immigration in National Population Projections of Selected EEC-Countries, Medium Variant, Medium and Long Term (per 1,000 of the 1985 midyear population)

Country	Year	EEC	Africa	Rest	Total	Total in % of total population	Total minus EEC
		x 1000					
Denmark	1986	25.7	4.6	86.7	117.0	2	2
Ireland	1985	196.4	-	36.0	232.4	7	1
U.Kingdom[a]	1984/86	754	99	883	1736	3[b]	2[b]
Belgium	1985	583.9	157.6	156.2	897.6	9	3
France[c]	1982	1577.9	1573.8	708.4	3680.1	7	4
F.R.Germany	1986	1364.7	145.1	3002.9	4512.7	7	5
Luxembourg[d]	1981	88.5	0.6	6.6	95.8	26[d]	4[d]
Netherlands	1986	161.5	128.4	262.6	552.5	4	3
Greece	1985	208.5	9.0	78.4	295.8	3	1
Italy	1985	220.5	-	202.5	423.0	1	0
Portugal	1986	22.5	37.8	26.6	87.0	1	1
Spain	1984	134.2	7.7	84.6	226.5	1	-

Sources: Eurostat (1988), CoE (1987) and Callovi (1988)

[a] based on results of labour force survey, average 1984-86
[b] average population as of June 1984, 1985 and 1986
[c] metropolitan
[d] foreigners as of 31-03-81, divided by total population per mid-April

TABLE 10:   Foreigners in EEC-Countries, in the Eighties

Region and country	Projected total fertility rates					
	1985	1990	1995	2000	2010	2020
Denmark[a]	1.45	1.50	1.50	1.50	1.50	1.50
Ireland[a]	2.49	2.10[e]	2.10	2.10	2.10	2.10
United Kingdom[d]	1.80	1.87	1.97	2.00	2.00	2.00
Belgium[a]	1.49	1.49	--	1.95	--	--
France[a]	1.82	1.79	1.79	1.79	1.80	1.80
Fed.Rep.Germany[a]	1.28	1.287	1.287	1.287	1.287	1.287
Luxembourg[b]	1.39	1.51	1.60	1.67	1.80	1.80
Netherlands[c]	1.50	1.60	1.63	1.65	1.65	1.65
Greece[a]	1.68	1.8	2.1	2.1	2.1	--
Italy[a]	1.42	1.32	1.32	1.32	1.32	1.32
Spain[a]	1.71[d]	1.73	1.73	1.73	1.73	1.73

[a] variant 1
[b] variant 2
[c] medium variant
[d] 1983
[e] 1991

Sources: K. Szabò (1988) for 1990-2020

TABLE 11: Projected Total Fertility Rates in National Projections of Selected EEC-Countries, 1985-2020

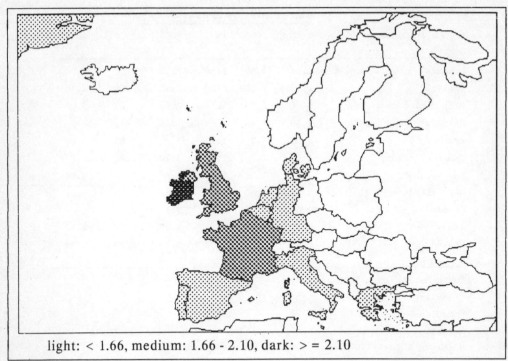

light: < 1.66, medium: 1.66 - 2.10, dark: > = 2.10

FIGURE 1:   Total Fertility Rate EEC-Countries, 1988 or latest available data

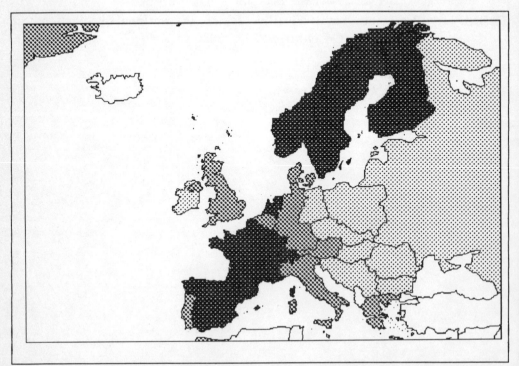

FIGURE 2:   Life Expectancy at Birth in Years: Females, European Countries, 1986 or latest available data

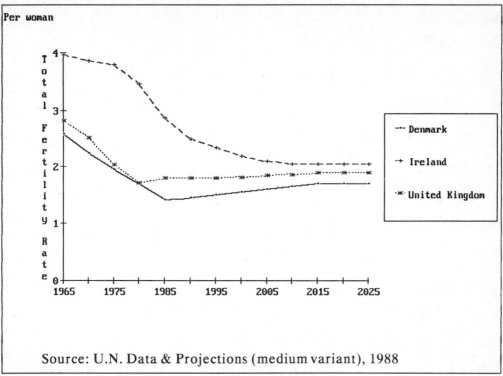

Source: U.N. Data & Projections (medium variant), 1988

FIGURE 3a: Northern Europe, Total Fertility Rate

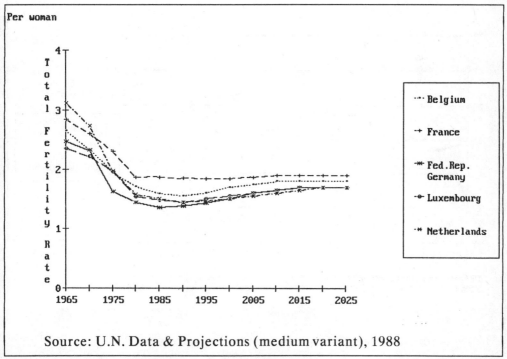

Source: U.N. Data & Projections (medium variant), 1988

FIGURE 3b: Western Europe, Total Fertility Rate

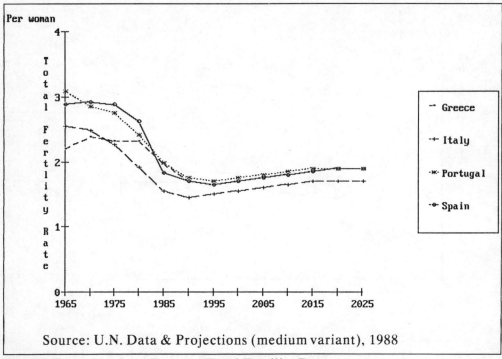

Source: U.N. Data & Projections (medium variant), 1988

FIGURE 3c: Southern Europe, Total Fertility Rate

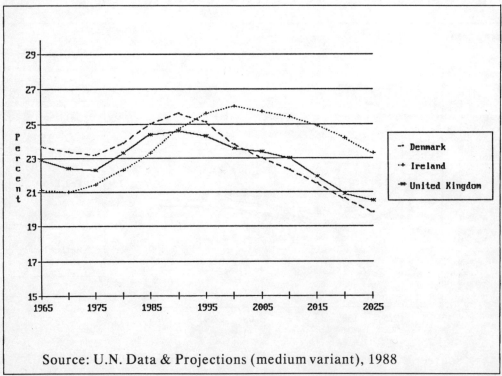

Source: U.N. Data & Projections (medium variant), 1988

FIGURE 4a: Northern Europe, Proportion of women aged 15 - 49

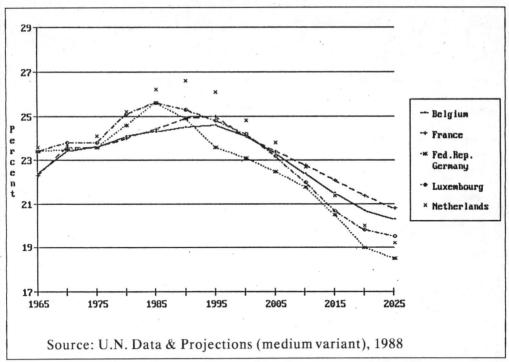

Source: U.N. Data & Projections (medium variant), 1988

FIGURE 4b: Western Europe, Proportion of women aged 15 - 49

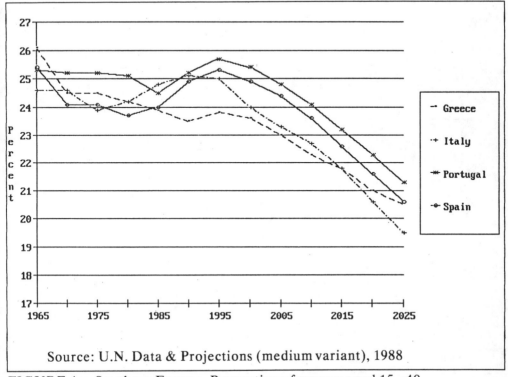

Source: U.N. Data & Projections (medium variant), 1988

FIGURE 4c: Southern Europe, Proportion of women aged 15 - 49

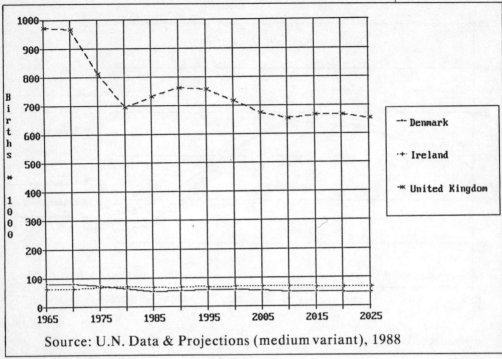

Source: U.N. Data & Projections (medium variant), 1988

FIGURE 5a: Northern Europe, Births

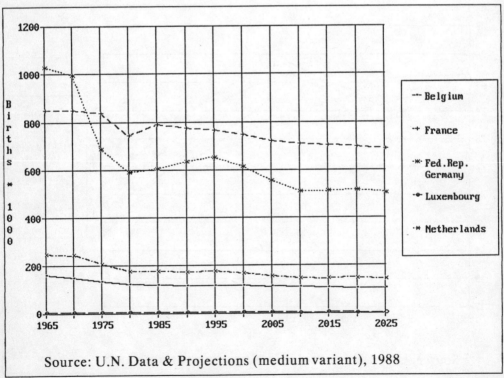

Source: U.N. Data & Projections (medium variant), 1988

FIGURE 5b: Western Europe, Births

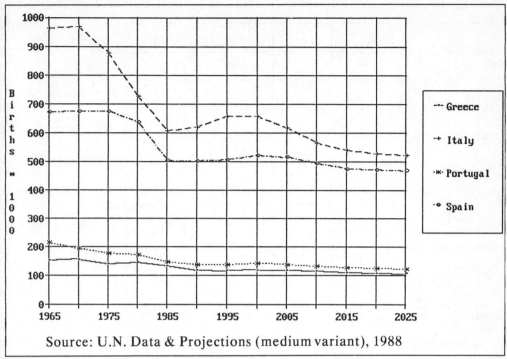

Source: U.N. Data & Projections (medium variant), 1988

FIGURE 5c: Southern Europe, Births

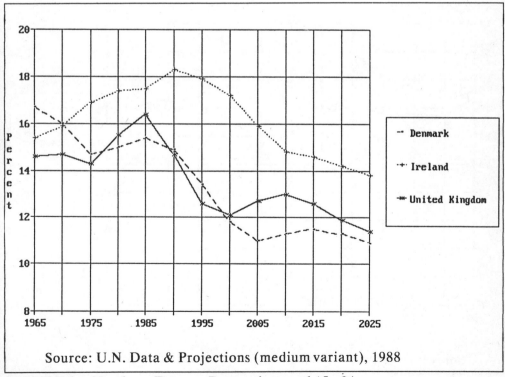

Source: U.N. Data & Projections (medium variant), 1988

FIGURE 6a: Northern Europe, Proportion aged 15 - 24

24

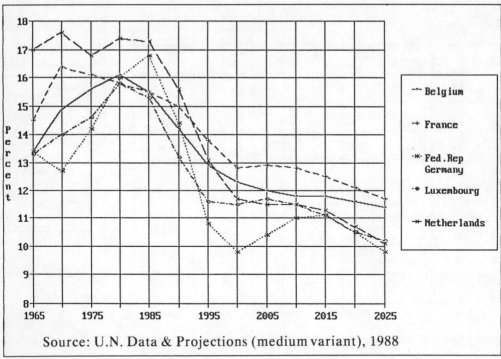

Source: U.N. Data & Projections (medium variant), 1988

FIGURE 6b: Western Europe, Proportion aged 15 - 24

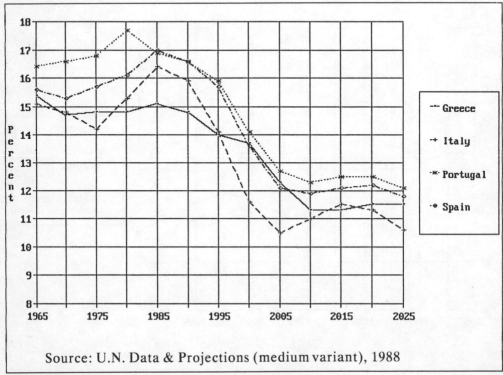

Source: U.N. Data & Projections (medium variant), 1988

FIGURE 6c: Southern Europe, Proportion aged 15 - 24

FOREIGNERS IN THE COUNTRIES OF THE EUROPEAN COMMUNITY - RECENT DEVELOPMENTS AND FUTURE TRENDS

Ulrich Mammey,
Federal Institute for Population Research,
Wiesbaden

This report deals with two aspects of foreign immigration in the countries of the European Community:

Firstly, recent numbers, proportions, structures and the development of the foreign population in the various countries are investigated`and, secondly, future trends of foreign immigration in the Community are looked upon.

1. RECENT FIGURES AND STRUCTURES

One should assume that the first part of this contribution could be carried out without any great difficulty compared with the always speculative look into the future, but several problems arise already when defining the terms immigration, immigrant and foreigner. Most of the countries follow the UN recommendation to define immigration inter alia by the length of stay - West-German official statistics do not so. In West-Germany foreigners are simply defined as not having a German passport (about 4.5 million persons), whereas in Britain, for instance, only 1.7 million inhabitants are foreigners according to this definition. The criterion of nationality to estimate the size of the foreign population and to compare it with that of other European countries is unsatisfactory. The criterion of the birth country, which was used in the last census in Britain to approach the immigrant population seems to be a more comparable measure. According to this definition, the number of foreigners was twice as large, namely 3.4 million. On the other hand, these figures include those British citizens who were born abroad, and exclude all the descendants of non-British citizens who were born in the United Kingdom. Some countries do not even have any emigration or immigration statistics, so that the number of immigrants can only be derived from censuses, which is the case in France.

What is the numerical dimension we are dealing with when talking about foreigners within a "Europe of the Twelve"? Summing up the absolute figures of each country (excepting Italy, for which no corresponding data is available) we get the total of 12.5 million persons. However, 4.8 million of them (or 38%) are citizens of one of the member states and therefore EC citizens. One quarter of the total are Europeans from non-member countries and 36% are from countries outside Europe.

Each of the countries concerned has its own immigration history. In some countries this history was predominantly influenced by their colonial policy, in others by the fact that in frontier areas a mix of two or more nationalities and often changing borders produced a population which was permanently on the move. Despite all the different immigration histories there was one prevailing reason for the migratory flows into Western European countries which started still very soon after the end of World War II, namely economic reasons. The national composition of these migrants, however, was and is still very often a reflection of historical relations between the countries.

This becomes apparent when the nationality structure of some selected countries is compared with the three fundamental groups of nationality which have been mentioned already, i.e. the members of EC countries, foreigners from European non-member countries and foreigners from non-European countries (figures 1 - 5):

The first example shall be the Netherlands. In this country the increase of the foreign population during the eighties from 420 000 to 570 000 was predominantly due to the growth of the non-European sector, but the number of Europeans from non-member countries is on the increase, too. The number of nationals from member countries remained relatively constant during the eighties. Due to the growing share of non-member foreigners, the proportion of foreigners from EC member countries is on the decrease from 38 % in 1979 to about 28% in 1987. About the same observation can be made in the case of Belgium. Although in this country the proportion of EC citizens is above average, it is clearly visible that their absolute number as well as their proportion are continuously going down. A similar observation can be made in the case of Denmark as well as in the case of the Federal Republic of Germany. Not only is the proportion of EC foreigners decreasing, but also their absolute number is going down or is at least stagnating. A special development can be observed in the case of Greece: All sectors are growing rather rapidly, although starting from a very low level of some 70 000 foreigners in 1979. The proportion of EC citizens has, however, been stagnating since 1982 on a level of about one third of the total foreign population.

For the rest of the EC countries no time series are available. The actual data on the percentage of foreigners within the total population as well as the division into the three nationality groups are shown in the following table:

Foreign population in the member countries of the European Community

Country (year)	Foreign population (1000)	% of total population	% of total foreign population from EC	Other Eur. countries	Non-Eur. countries
France (1982)	3680.1	6,8	42,9	8,1	49,0
Netherlands (1987)	568.0	3,9	28,1	32,6	39,3
Belgium (1987)	853.2	8,6	63,1	11,2	25,8
Luxembourg (1981)	95.8	26,2	92,5	4,0	3,5
United Kingdom (1981)	1736.0	3,0	43,4	7,0	49,6
Denmark (1987)	128.3	2,5	20,8	46,5	32,8
Greece (1987)	193.4	1,9	57,4	10,1	32,6
Portugal (1987)	89.8	0,9	26,6	2,0	71,4
Spain (1987)	334.9	0,9	57,7	6,9	35,4
F.R.Germany (1987)	4630.2	7,6	29,8	55,1	15,2
Ireland (1981)	232.4	6,8	84,5	0,0	15,5
Italy	.	.	.	.	.
Total	12542.1	.	32,7	25,8	41,5

Source: Eurostat, Demographic Statistics, Luxembourg 1988 and 1989

TABLE 1

In France with a percentage of foreigners of 6.8 nearly one half of all foreigners are from non-European countries, mainly from the Maghreb region. Luxemburg is the country with the highest proportion of foreign population amounting to more than 26%. Nearly all of them are nationals of an EC member state. In the United Kingdom, the overwhelming share of the EC citizens is from Ireland, whereas vice versa most of the foreigners from other EC countries in Ireland are nationals of the United Kingdom. Another extreme feature of the UK is the extraordinary share of those foreigners originating from overseas - a heritage of the British colonial history. An even higher proportion of foreigners from non-European countries can be observed in the case of Portugal, although on a much lower absolute level.

EUROSTAT - the statistical office of the European Community - does not provide any figures on Italy, but Italian statisticians guess that more than 1 million foreigners are living in their country - a growing share of them coming from Africa.

2. FUTURE TRENDS

It is the intention of the EC-Commission to improve the free movement of labour within the "Europe of the Twelve". In view of the Commission the mobility of skilled workers, however, has to be balanced in such a way that a more or less homogeneous distribution of the migrants according to their areas of origin and destination is guaranteed, as it is to be feared that certain member states or regions will suffer excessive losses of skilled workers (Lorenz, M., 1989). How should these fears be judged?

Recently, two demographers from Amsterdam, Penninx and Muus (1989), published an article on the possible population movements within the Community after 1992. They come to the following conclusion: "The presence of large numbers of unemployed nationals both of the European Community and from outside, with a low level of skills, means that even if demands for labour were to increase, provision for it could easily be made without immigration". They consider immigration of skilled migrant workers from non-European countries to be more likely.

The authors draw their conclusions from a publication of the seventies (Böhning, W. R., 1972) and from own considerations. Böhning compared speculations about the massive influx of immigrants which took place before the free movement of labour between the states of the EC came about in 1968 with the actual movements afterwards. As we all know, the overwhelming number of immigrants did not come from the member countries but from countries outside the Community.

Secondly, the authors design a typology of migrants which is made up "from a combination of categories based on government policy on admission (...) and on sociological considerations relevant to the motives, intentions and environment of the individual migrants". For the individual categories of migrants assumptions have been formulated on both the macro and micro level.

The authors' findings are as follows:

The demand for unskilled labour has declined radically, whereas a lack of skilled labour has developed. In the event of an economic boom, immigration of skilled labour is more likely from non-Community countries. However, the extent of immigration of this kind is considered not to be comparable to that of the previous labour migration of the 1960s.

Not so much dependent on changes in the economic climate are secondary migrations of families and marriage partners. Anyway, the peak of these movements is thought to have passed already.

Although the number of refugees and asylum seekers has increased in all Community countries, there is no common policy in this respect. It can be assumed that this kind of migration pressure will continue to be high in the future - independent from the existence of the common market as from 1993. "The number of requests for asylum, and acceptances, will primarily depend on the Community's common policy on refugees and asylum".

The question of illegals is regarded as a function of the system of immigration control. Illegals can be rejected asylum seekers, migrant workers who have lost their right of residence for various reasons, tourists who did not return, and family members without the right of family reunion. Without a labour permit, they are forced to live on illegal work or on the support of their families.

As stressed already in the case of asylum seekers, it must however be emphasized again that the number of illegals will be independent from the existence of the common market. Regarding regulation of foreign immigration from third countries, the decision of the EC Commission of June 1988 regarding the coordination of national immigration policies will be much more important.

All in all, the authors come to the conclusion that no more major migration can be expected between the member states .

These findings and hypotheses may be supported more or less by observations of immigration trends in the Federal Republic of Germany and will be more or less comparable with the situation in the other member countries:

Already Böhning (1972) measured the effects of the free movement of labour during the first years after its introduction in 1968. Comparing these effects with movements into non-member states, as for instance Switzerland, he came to the conclusion that the demand for labour was the predominant reason for the increase of labour immigration and not the new EC legislation. In the case of Germany - as can be seen in Figure 6 - the increase of the number of EC-foreigners between 1968 and 1974 was the continuation of a process which came into effect already six or more years earlier. The countries with the greatest contribution during this period were the then non-member states Greece, Portugal and Spain. Recruitment agreements with these countries had already existed for a number of years. The only member country which was a significant source of immigrant workers was Italy - the Federal Republic's first recruitment country. The number of foreigners from the Benelux-countries as well as from France - member states at that time - did not increase significantly. The introduction of free movement for Greeks, in effect from the beginning of 1988, brought about a small increase in the number of Greek citizens in Germany. The number of immigrating Greeks doubled to 33 000 persons in 1988 as compared to 1987. This increase can be interpreted as the result of some kind of removed barrier effect which will not continue in the coming years.

One of the objectives of the European Community is to attain an increasing similarity of the living conditions and a broad supply of places of work in all regions of the Community. This policy has been successful insofar as obviously many citizens of the former recruitment countries Italy, Greece, Spain and Portugal, which became members of the Community in the meantime, had the possibility to return to their home countries (Figure 6).

A look back into the past may enlighten what could happen in the future: As the numbers of citizens of the former recruitment countries are decreasing, the numbers of those from the Benelux, from the United Kingdom and Ireland as well as from France are on the increase. How can this seeming contradiction be explained? Obviously there are two different developments overlapping each other at present. On one hand some of the former un- and semi-skilled guestworkers are leaving the country whereas, on the other, more highly-skilled and specialized employees are entering. Therefore in the chart the broad ribbon of the Italians, for instance, must be divided into two sectors: a slim ribbon of the "elite" which is growing broader like that of the French or British on the top, and another one for the lower levels of skill which is fading away in the course of time. For semi- and unskilled labour moving into another country of the Twelve will become less attractive since modernization in the countries at the periphery of Europe is resulting in better opportunities of getting a job and in adjusting the level of income. Moving across the borders of the Twelve will become more and more the characteristics of the increasing number of highly skilled employees of multinational companies.

The last chart (Figure 7) provides an overall view of the immigrants in the Federal Republic by categories of employment, i.e. immigrants who are employed or not employed. Regarding the immigrants in total during the eighties, it is obvious that the number of employed immigrants rather declined whereas the immigrants not employed tripled since 1983. Taking the immigrants from EC countries separately, we can see that both employed and not employed immigrants are on the increase during the last years. Immigrating

Turks, however, are predominantly not employed - obviously a result of an efficient immigration control.

A new feature of European migration are pensioners moving from the North to the Mediterranean - at least for temporary stays. As yet, the right of residence is bound to employment, but it is likely that sooner or later this right will be extended to those whose maintenance is ensured. Europe growing together economically and sociopolitically will result in higher mobility of the elderly.

All in all, there will be no mass migration between the EC countries after 1992 - if all the signs are to be believed. Also for demographic reasons, there is no European country with any resources for emigration. Much more likely will be an increase of migration pressure from non-member states. But this is a different subject!

3. BIBLIOGRAPHY

Böhning, W. R. (1972): *The Migration of Workers in the United Kingdom and the European Community.* London

Lorenz, M. (1989): *Binnenmarkt verändert viel.* In: Bundesarbeitsblatt 2. Bonn

Penninx, R., Muus, P. (1989): *No Limits for Migration after 1992? The Lessons of the Past and a Reconnaissance of the Future.* In: International Migration, XXVII, 373 - 388

4. FIGURES

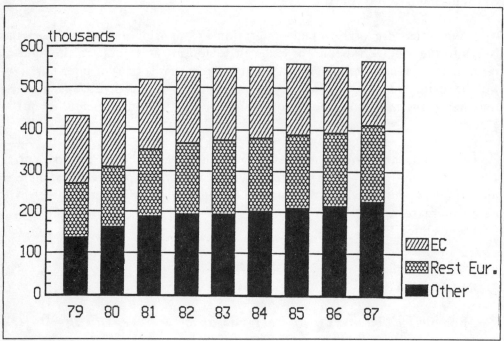

FIGURE 1a: Foreign Population in Netherlands (absolute figures)

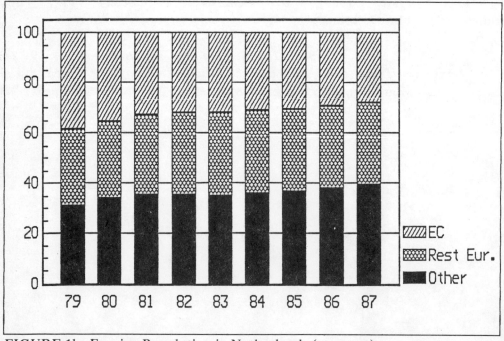

FIGURE 1b: Foreign Population in Netherlands (per cent)

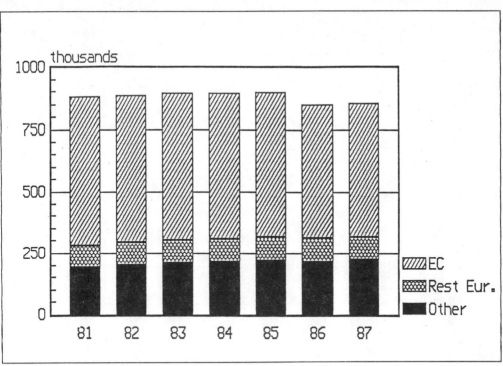

FIGURE 2a: Foreign Population in Belgium (absolute figures)

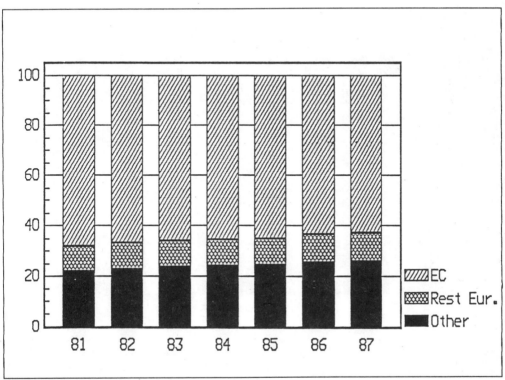

FIGURE 2b: Foreign Population in Belgium (per cent)

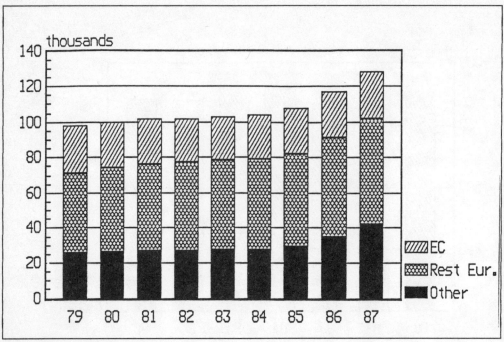

FIGURE 3a: Foreign Population in Denmark (absolute figures)

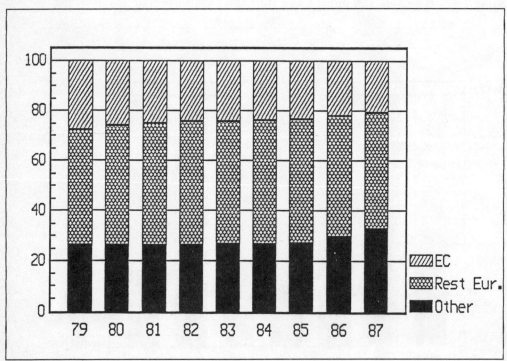

FIGURE 3b: Foreign Population in Denmark (per cent)

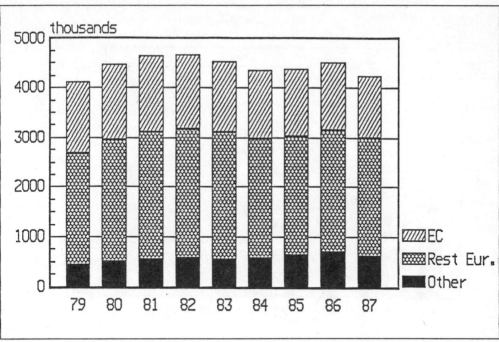

FIGURE 4a: Foreign Population in F.R. Germany (absolute figures)

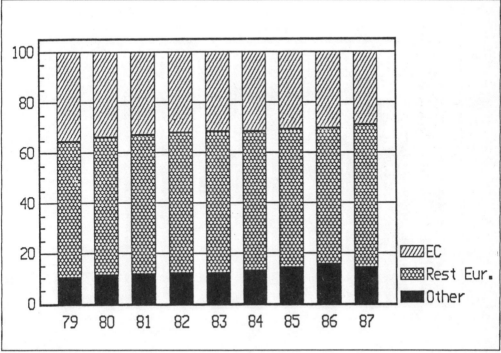

FIGURE 4b: Foreign Population in F.R. Germany (per cent)

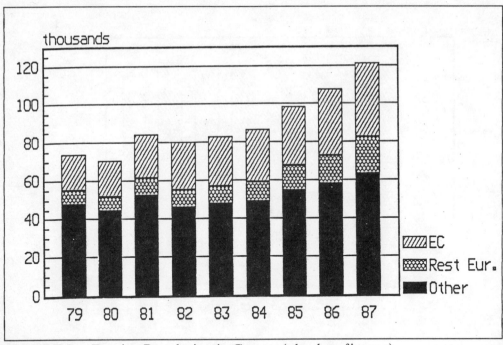

FIGURE 5a: Foreign Population in Greece (absolute figures)

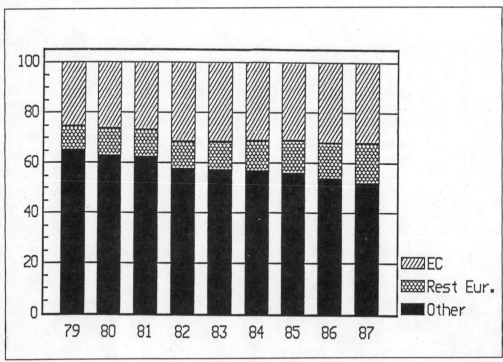

FIGURE 5b: Foreign Population in Greece (per cent)

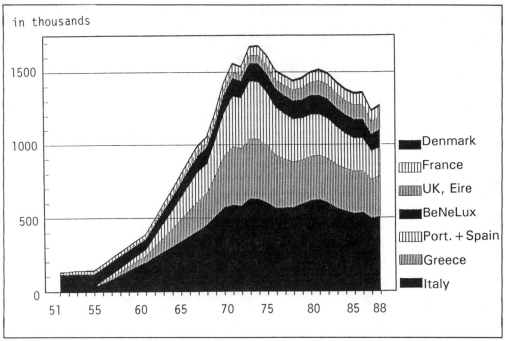

FIGURE 6: Citizens form EC Member States as of 1989 in the F.R. Germany

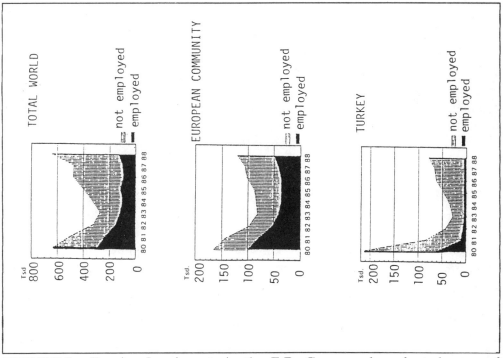

FIGURE 7: Foreign Immigrants in the F.R. Germany by selected areas of origin, 1980 - 1990

EUROPEAN EMPLOYMENT:
CHANGES IN STRUCTURE AND QUALITY

Robert M. Lindley
Institute of Employment Research
University of Warwick, Coventry, CV4 7AL

0. INTRODUCTION

This note draws on the work of an international comparative study (1). Its focus, however, shifts from quantitative changes in the structure of employment to more qualitative changes, especially those dealing with the skill content of jobs. It further concentrates upon the so-called 'intermediate' part of the occupational spectrum. This is because the intermediate range of skills is of particular interest in the study of how demographic, social, economic and technological factors affect the structure of employment and access to the jobs within it. The mix of educat
ion, training and work experience involved in preparing for such occupations varies quite considerably between occupations and countries.

Many intermediate occupations have expanded rapidly during the post-war period, accompanied by the emergence of new occupations. As the latter crystallise out of the job structure they are subject to an increasing formalisation of educational and training requirements. Longer-standing occupation also adapt their requirements to changing conditions. Projections of occupational employment of the UK suggest the growth will be greatest among associate professional and technical occupations (Institute for Employment Research, 1988/89).

Some intermediate occupations jostle for position between the craftor equivalent skilled non-manual occupations and the professions. Some primarily emerge on the edge of a profession where an expertise becomes separable from a wider body of professional knowledge and skill and the economic, organisational and technological environment encourages a rejigging of the job structure. Other intermediate occupations develop primarily from lower level jobs, though they too may eventually encroach upon the traditional preserves of higher level jobs or the professions.

1. BROAD STRUCTURE

As regards the more quantitatively based conclusions of the study, these were as follows.

i.   The growth of new forms and areas of employment will fail to compensate sufficiently for the loss of jobs elsewhere and the growth of labour supply. Assuming that national policies remain broadly on the lines adopted during the mid-1980s, the most optimistic outcome is that European unemployment will decline only slowly.

ii.   The industrial structure will continue to change in favour of the service sector as conventionally classified but the changes will not be as marked as that experienced over the 1975 - 1985 period. First, after the adjustments made during the recession, European manufacturing industry is more competitive and overall will experience a slower decline in employment. Second, the growth of services will be hampered by the effects of restrictive budgetary policies upon the development of public services.

iii.   The main projected areas of employment growth common to all five countries are business and related services, tourism and leisure activities, and health care. There are significant differences between countries in the prospect of manufacturing employment.

iv.   The occupations most likely to expand are the more highly qualified groups: those particularly associated with industrial growth - financial and business specialists, recreation professions, and health care professions; those likely to increase their employment in many industries - managers and supervisors; and those whose employment is fairly concentrated in less buoyant industries but where occupational shares within those industries are rising - engineers, scientists and the intermediate technical occupations.

v.   Associated with there projected industrial and occupational changes are further increases in the employment of women and further (modest) reductions in hours worked per year by full-time employees. Self-emplyment is expected to rise in threee of the countries, tending to stabilise in the other two.

2. QUALITATIVE ASPECTS OF OCCUPATIONAL CHANGE

Against this rough aggregate picture it is possible to consider the case-study evidence. It is worth stressing, however, that case studies are difficult to set into perspective. Moreover, in an international comparative context the danger of making too much out of unrepresentative cases is compounded by the danger of emphasising the inter-country differences when in fast the intra-country differences are of equal or more significance.

The range of evidence considered by the individual country studies (see Chapter 3 in each study cited in the references) varies quite markedly and this, to a considerable degree, is due to variations in the evidence available. It also reflects the different national debates about new technology, flexibility and employment. However, all the country studies refer to the qualitative changes in job content of those industrial-occupational categories most affected by the introduction of new technology in production. The planning, control, adjustment, maintenance and repair functions have been greatly affected by the progressive reduction of employment in the production and materials handling functions. It is clear, moreover, that very real choices face management in devising occupational structures to implement even the same production technology. An analogous situation arises from the impact of information technology on office-based activities concerning general administration through highly specialised technical work in engineering research, design and development.

Turning to the case-study evidence on changing job content, a combination of 'stylised facts and related issues' emerges rather than clear international contrasts. These are quite consistent with the analysis of more aggregate data and are summarised briefly below. Specific reference to a particular country will only be made where there seems to be either a marked divergence from the position being adopted or an especially strong example of the point being made.

2.1 Occupations concerned with planning, monitoring and control - notably, managers and supervisors

Changes in job content which will accompany the further expansion of management jobs will refrect the wider range of competence expected of managers and the need to take responsibility for a more complex process. The latter will use more capital and fewer people but with personnel engaged on more demanding tasks and involving greater autonomy. The requirement for broader expertise will affect general managers and specialists alike with the former acquiring greater technical knowledge and the latter, more business skills.

Responsibility for a greater mix of capital equipment and skilled employees will also characterise the supervisory occupation where more emphasis will be laid upon communication with and the motivation of employees. This aspect has been ignored by some commentators who have expected supervisors to decline simply with the number of semi-skilled and unskilled personnel under them.

2.2 The relationship between higher and intermediate professions

This issue concerns the relationships both between long-established occupations (doctor/nurse, scientist/laboratory technician, etc.) and between relatively new occupations (software engineer/programmer, design engineer/technician/draughtsperson, manager/data processing specialist). In many of these linked occupations. changes in product demand, labour market conditions, and vocational education are creating situations in which significant adjustments are already taking place in some countries. Relative salary costs and shortages of certain higher-level skills combined with the development of technological aids to decision-making indicate the potential for further changes (e.g. in health care) subject to institutional restraints.

In addition, in certain areas of the economy there seems to be scope for the emergence of new higher and intermediate professional groups. For example (Italy, pp. 45 - 46), the development of tourism and leisure activities need not be associated with a continuation of temporary, sometimes seasonal, low skilled and low paid employment. Aiming at higher quality and a wider range of service generates a demand for more professionally qualified entrepreneurs, managers and local administrators, supported by a cadre of skilled personnel. The latter may work behind the scenes or be in direct contact with the customer (e.g. in providing tourist/travel information, instruction in recreational pursuits, supervision of customer relations in hotel, catering and recreational establishments). The speed with which such service industries move toward the 'high value added' end of their product market clearly determines the rate of growth of the more skilled occupations. It is also, however, determined by the rate at which appropriate new professional roles are identified and the relevant training is provided.

2.3   Other non-manual occupations

This group is dominated by clerical, secretarial and sales occupations. Some of these personnel are directly involved with customers in areas where attempts are being made to improve the quality of customer service. There the job content is placing greater stress on the combination of a higher level of product knowledge, inter-personal communication skills, keyboard skills and software knowledge needed to use the financial/sales information system, and wider commercial awareness.

In other respects, though, there seems to be some uncertainty about the net impact of organisational and technological change upon these occupations. It is generally agreed that many routine clerical tasks and the supervisory roles attached to them will be abolished with the widespread establishment and use of machine-readable data bases. The entry and interrogation of data will be organised much more efficiently but just how far supervisors, managers and other intermediate and higher professional staff will reduce their need for clerical and secretarial assistance remains to be seen. The scope for more complex analysis and presentation of data and the ability to create higher quality documentation is likely to increase the demand for certain clerical/secretarial staff. These will have higher levels of literac and numeracy, greater knowledge of the business and its information system, and skills in the use of software for word-processing, statistical analysis and graphics.

The above developments must also be considered in the light of two further factors. First, employment in these occupations is likely to benefit from the continuing growth of the service sector where the nature and size of many of its enterprises limit the economies of scale obtainable. Second, the quality considerations mentioned above in relation to customer service combine with efficiency arguments to create a demand for more flexible personnel. They should be able to switch from counter service to liaising with suppliers to carrying out supporting clerical and secretarial tasks. This is an emerging form of multi-skilled and multi-functional office-based occupation which receives less attention than does its manual craft counterpart (see below).

Thus whilst the net effect of these changes upon the numbers of clerical, secretarial and sales staff is highly uncertain, the content of the average job will tend to rise quite substantially (UK, p. 59).

2.4   Skilled production occupations

The fate of skilled craftsmen seems to be the crucial issue in considering the implementation of new technology. The possible consequences are (a) abolition of the job; (b) de-skilling to a large degree (e.g. to a machine-minding or materials handling function); (c) re-skilling where previous knowledge is transferred to a new context requiring some re-training (e.g. transfer to maintenance from production); (d) multi-skilling where, typically, the need for a wider craft-based competence involves the acquisition of complementary skills in electronics; and (e) up-grading to the status of technician/programmer/complex keyboard operator which exploits previous knowledge but involves substantial re-training or recruitment of qualified staff.

The development of the multi-skilled, multi-funktional, worker is highlighted in the case-study evidence for all countries (see, especially, France, p. 30; Italy, pp. 41 - 42; Netherlands, p. 31; UK, p. 60). A worker who deploys, for example, mechanical and electronics skills and deals with production, regulation of equipment and minor rpairs would fall into this category. Similar attention is paid to the specialised maintenance and repair functions employing highly skilled craftsmen. However, the introduction of new technology generally creates far fewer such jobs than it destroys or de-skills traditional craft jobs engaged in production (Germany, pp. 37 - 42). The extent of up-grading has evidently become the litmus test of enlightened management: how the numerically controlled machine is programmed and by whom is a noteworthy example. But the evidence on the relative costs of alternative strategies as opposed to their feasibility in terms of the technical and training requirements is extremely limited. The emerging division of labour between skilled manual workers and more highly qualified technical personnel at the point of technological transition is insufficiently monitored and understood at national level to allow for a satisfactory explanation of international differences.

2.5 Management control versus technological necessity as determinants of job content and occupational structure

The above point implies that it would also be premature to generalise on the much debated issue of how far employers seek out technologies and choose modes of implementation which increase their control over labour as the principal aim. Nonetheless, the introduction of information technology (in its widest sense) does present a praticularly important opportunity for examining this issue. Its flexibility would seem to offer the potential for a much greater variation of economically acceptable management choices than with other major technologies.

3. INTERMEDIATE SKILLS

The above discussion of developments in the structure of employment in several European countries has several implications for education and training policies. First, the emergence of a stronger intermediate skill base is probably a prerequisite for successful economic development in the decades ahead. Second, this would raise the average quality of employment opportunities, injecting into the middle of the job hierarchy a higher level of performance and reward. Third, the adoption of such and employment strategy implies the adoption of a product market strategy which shifts the organisation further toward the higher value added end of its existing market(s) or into new high value added markets.

The education and training of those with intermediate skills lies at the conjunction of a number of debates in the field of human resources. For it is in this area of the job structure where the appropriate mix between (and meanings of) 'education' and 'training', 'general' and 'specific' training, initial and continuing training, off-the-job and on-the-job training appear to be especially debatable. This leads to corresponding disagreement about the strategies for funding and supplying different parts of the education and training cycle.

Overall, however, promoting the emergence of a larger intermediate skill base would place additional pressure on a system of education and training such as Britain's at its weakest points as they affect attainment, opportunity and continuation. Britain has embraced neither mass upper-secondary eduction nor widely available training in intermediate skills (Table 1). A wariness of relying upon extended schooling to provide an appropriate mix of education and general vocational training has left it with a combination of schemes and specific training for the majority of young people. The general element of training under schemes has continually to be defended against the demands for specific relevance to the job or work experience on hand. The certification process itself is in danger of becoming too much the creature of internal rater than external labour markets and of pandering to low levels of attainment rather then promoting high levels (2). The British system has thus encouraged a early entry to the labour market similar to that of Germany but without the provision of employer-based high quality training to accompany it.

	Full Time Education	Apprenticeship, part-time, etc.	Total
Germany	51	46	97
Japan	90	0	90
United States	87	-	88
Netherlands	76	10	86
Belgium	78	8	86
Sweden	83 2)	2	85
Switzerland	27	55	82
Austria	34	44	78
Canada	76	-	76
France	65	10	75
Norway	74	1	75
Denmark	68	6	74
Italy 3)	47	23	70
Australia	46	20 4)	66
United Kingdom	30	35 5)	65
Spain	49	-	49
New Zealand	46	0	46
Portugal	38	3	41

Source: OECD (1988), p. 72.

Notes: 1) Figures are percentages of total population aged 17.
            2) Two-year upper-secondary courses.
            3) 1981 figures.
            4) Mainly part-time technical education.
            5) Including FE private and public part-time study and YTS.

TABLE 1:   Educational Enrolment of 17 Years Old (ca. 1984)

The problem with the job content associated with emerging patterns of intermediate skills is that it requires a higher level of general training and a longer span of vocational educational and training (VET) integrated with work experience. This makes it even less attractive for employers individually to provide the opportunities for training as part of an employment contract. The response to this may be to seek to galvanise employer collective commitment. The Experience of British training in the post-war period suggest, however, that this is a lost cause. Even when statutory backing was given through the industrial training boards (ITBs), the system in many industries settled for trying to persuade employers to do sufficient specific training rather than identifying primarily general training for support (Lindley, 1983). And when ITBs tried to increase the breadth and quality of training via placing the stress on general training, they were frustrated by the reactions of employers who were either reluctant to raise quality in the first place or acquiesced but then reduced quantity at a later stage.

The notion that industry is the place for general as well as specific industrial training has had a powerful influence upon the development of British policy. The rationale for it has been to ensure relevance and this has its components of marginal and hidden curricula. The overall curricula arguments for the sort of British practice common to many production industries sit uncomfortably with both the much broader conception which underpins the German system and the very different division of responsibility characterising the American system.

However, a shift away from relying upon the internal labour markets of organisations to foster investment in 'intermediate' human capital is likely to be required in those European countries which have successfully managed to achieve this so far. Those still struggling to make the grade should have cause to reflect on the feasibility of the strategy in the changing labour market conditions of the 1990s. Educational and training institutions would then play a larger part in providing VET and the state and individual a larger part in funding it.

4. COMPLETION OF THE EUROPEAN INTERNAL MARKET

Problems of maintaining existing employer investment in intermediate skills where it is already high and increasing it where it is relatively low may thus coincide with a period of greater 'trade' in intermediate skills. It is worth noting in this context a potentially very significant effect of completion of the internal market.

Tax-subsidy regimes operated by European governments differ markedly. Those which directly affect the wedge between basic input costs and market prices can, in principle, be manipulated to a considerable degree in order to gain a cost advantage over a competitor. The impact of greater product market competition may well cause governments to reconsider their current practices regarding input markets, especially if given the encouragement of liberal 'competition between regulations' approach to these matters by the Commission. Public expenditure on education and training could become the most significant industrial subsidy to be legitimised as the Community emerges from the completion process.

Completion of the European internal market will increase organisational flexibility regarding the location of different corporate functions and relationships with suppliers. This makes it necessary for each Community country to scrutinise the environment it offers to business. From the point of view of the labour market, Lindley (1989) has distinguished the 'subsidy regime', 'regulation regime' and 'human capital regime'. Debate on the programme for completion has now shifted to some degree from the first of these to the second because of the announcement of the Commission's agenda for the 'Social Charter'.

In terms of the behaviour of companies, especially those operating at international level, it appears, however, that increasing importance is being attached to the human capital regime and its associated informational infrastructure (market conditions for the generation and application of intellectual property including R&D, business information services, and related physical infrastructures, especially telecommunications). Consideration of this aspect, moreover, points to the interaction between the three regimes. Particularly significant is the subsidy regime pertaining to vocational education and training (VET). Rather than adopting a more permissive attitude to industrial subsidies, an option for Community policy would be to promote conditions in the markets for VET which will help to achieve the quality strategy.

The regulation regime covering VET is also important. The measures to promote a single labour market include the mutual recognition of qualifications and other arrangements to facilitate access to national labour markets. The Social Charter will no doubt aim to give workers rights to initial and continuing VET. But these activities are organised in very different ways by the member states. To the extent that there are 'markets' for VET, the ground rules for the explicit and implicit subsidy regimes underpinning, indeed, dominating them, will need to be given much more attention by the Community. This is because the human capital intensity of economic activity will increase in the long run and subsidies to the creation and utilisation of human capital are likely to assume much greater importance in creating and maintaining European-wide product and labour markets and ensuring world-wide competitiveness of European industry.

5. CONCLUDING COMMENTS

This paper offers four broad working hypotheses relating especially to intermediate skills. They have strong policy implications but there is a need for more conclusive research (see Lindley 1989a for further analysis of the British case).

The first derives from the (admittedly very tentative) evidence on the relationships between occupation, job content and qualification. This suggests that there is a problem of over-qualification at the low skill end of the occupational spectrum (this is clear in the case of women) which co-exists with a more specific (and internationally variable) problem of under-qualification and skill shortages in certain intermediate occupations (notably, technicians and multi-skilled craftsmen), the more highly qualified technological specialists, and management.

The implication is that there is a smaller shortage of unskilled and semi-skilled jobs for the less able members of the workforce than appears from the unemployment statistics. The main shortage could well be for skilled manual and non-manual jobs for those in the intermediate and higher ability ranges. Note that this is expressed in terms of ability rather than qualification. A shortage of skilled jobs for able people co-exists with a shortage of those skills which are most efficiently acquired by able people. The response to the latter shortage is to limit the growth of such jobs in the development of new occupational structures which further exacerbates the former shortage. Despite recent policy innovations, it is doubtful whether employers individually will have sufficient incentive to remedy this situation, or whether voluntary collective action will meet the scales of the problem and approach it sufficiently from the long-term point of view.

Second, successful European economies will extend and intensify their intermediate skills base across a wide range of production and service industries. This will raise the quality of employment overall, reduce inefficiency and inequity due to educational crowding out, and improve the performance of those in occupations above and blow the intermediate skill level in the job hierarchy.

Third, the higher quality VET required to achieve the above will produce strains even in countries with a strong employer commitment to broadly-based training. The larger the investment required, the greater the risk of breaches in collective commitment. The chances of unbalancing the training effort are also higher if an element of international mobility develops in European markets for intermediate skills.

Finally, there is likely to be increasing pressure to externalise more of the education and training function, despite the philosophy of 'the place for training is in industry'. This reflects the needs of an increasingly fluid or flexible labour market from both employer and employee perspectives. The creation of a much more developed market for educational and training opportunities would widen the scope for providing individuals with much greater discretion in preparing themselves for work. It would involve an increasing separation of the provision of vocational education and training from the possession of an employment contract. But it would require the wider certification of training in order to create marketable 'commodities' recognised by both employers and workers. It would also involve renegotiating the division of responsibilities currently being pursued by the British government for supplying and funding VET for intermediate skills.

Thus when consindering the prospects for European labour demand, it is important to stress the qualitative changes in progress. Structural deficiencies in the markets for labour, education and training might impede the growth of employment in higher value added activities. Skill enrichment options associated with organisational and technical change may turn out to be infeasible because of constraints on the supply of skills, particularly in the intermediate range. Demographically-determined declines in the numbers of young people entering the labour market serve to reinforce the significance of this area of policy.

6. NOTES

1. This was funded by the Commission of the European Communities (Directorate General for Employment, Social Affairs and Education, DGV). I am grateful for helpful discussions with fellow participants: Henri Nadel and Laurent Schwab (France); Kurt Vogler-Ludwig (Germany); Bruno Contini (Italy); Tammo Oegama and Chris Van der Vegt (Netherlands); Rob Wilson and Derek Bosworth (United Kingdom); Andrew Chapman, John Morley and Klaus Keading (Commission DGV); and Anne Houtman (Eurostat). The views expressed in this paper are, however, my responsibility and should not necessarily be attributed to the other participants. For ease of identification, each of the country studies is cited in the text according to country rather than author(s) with the full details given in the list of references.

2. See Prais (1989) of a discussion of this in a European context.

7. REFERENCES

Contini, Bruno et al. (Italy 1987). *New Form and New Areas of Employment Growth: Italy.* Brussels: Commission of the European Communities.

Department of Employment (1988). *Employment in the 1990s.* London: HMSO.

Institute for Employment Research (1988/98). *Review of the Economy and Employment.* Coventry: University of Warwick.

Lindley, R.M. (1983). *'Active Manpower Policy'. Industrial Relations in Britain: Past Trends and Future Developments.* Ed. G.S. Bain. Oxford: Blackwell, 339-360

Lindley, R.M. (1987). *New Forms and New Areas of Employment Growth.* Brussels: Commission of the European Communities.

Lindley, R.M. (1989). *'Fiscal Policy, Labour Market Strategies and 1992'.* Conference on 'Mercato del Lavoro, Disoccupazione e Politiche di Intervento'.

Lindley, R.M. (1989a). *'Interactions in the markets for Education, Training and Labour: A European Prospective on Intermediate Skills'.* Training Agency Seminar on International Comparisons of Vocational Education and Training for Intermediate Skills, Manchester, September 1989.

Nadel, Henri and Laurent Schwab (France 1987). *New Forms and New Areas of Employment Growth: France.* Brussels: Commission of the European Communities.

OECD (1987). *Structural Adjustment and Economic Performance.* Paris: OECD

Oegema, Tammo and Chris von der Vegt (Netherlands 1987). *New Forms and New Areas of Employment Growth: The Netherlands.* Brussels: Commission of the European Communities.

Prais, S.J. (1989). *'How Europe would see the new British initiative for standardising vocational qualifications'.* National Institute Economic Review, No. 129 (August), 52-54.

Vogler-Ludwig, Kurt (Germany 1986). *New Forms and New Areas of Employment Growth: Germany*. Brussels: Commission of the European Communities.

Wilson, R.A. and D.L. Bosworth (UK 1987). *New Forms and New Areas of Employment Growth: United Kingdom*. Brussels: Commission of the European Communities.

DEMOGRAPHIC DEVELOPMENT AND THE LABOUR MARKET - GERMAN AND EUROPEAN PERSPECTIVES

Friedrich Buttler
Institut für Arbeitsmarkt- und Berufsforschung
Nuremberg

INTRODUCTION

This paper is concerned deals with the supply-side of the labour market, and, in doing so, it is complementary to the previous paper on prospects of the labour demand. Unfortunately, I will not be able to extend my detailed analysis concerning the FRG to the other EC member states. Therefore, as regards the European perspective, I have to confine myself to some rather brief comments.

The Institute of Employment Research (IAB) of the Federal Employment Services is not specialized in demographic studies. It rather uses the analysis of demographic developments as a tool for medium-term and long-term labour market forecasting. In doing so, it is necessary to translate demographic processes into labour-market processes, and the key concept to be used here is the development of the labour force potential.

1. COMPONENTS OF THE LABOUR FORCE POTENTIAL

The "potential" labour force is the maximum labour force that can be mobilized within an economy during periods of high labour demand (boom period). At each moment it is the result of three components influencing it: the "demographic", the "behavioural", and the "migration" component. Consequently, the labour force potential changes over time because of the development of the components.

In the framework of the labour market balance (Fig. 1) for the FRG 1970 - 2010, the relationship between the demand for labour force potential can be readily understood. The realized demand in each period is shown by the lowest curve (employed). The labour force potential can be defined here by summing up the employed, the registered unemployed and the labour reserve. In Figure 1 the data for the employed persons stem from a provisional adjustment of the Central Statistical Office's occupational data to the population census 1987, the data for the registered unemployed are published by the Federal

Employment Services, and hidden unemployment is estimated by the IAG (for methodological details see MittAG 4/1987, p. 387-409).

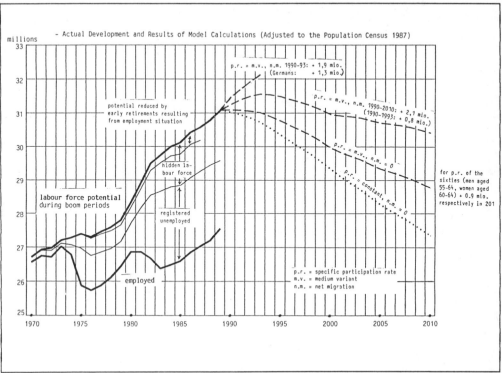

FIGURE 1:   Labour Market Balance 1970 - 2010 (Klauder 1990)

Figure 1 exposes four different time paths for the future development of the potential labour force. The lowest line is calculated on the assumption that only the demographic component is becoming effective, i.e. constant participation rates and net migration being zero. The above lines include variations of the labour force participation rate following a medium variant (m.v.) of the IAB model (lower dotted line), and additionally they admit positive net migration (upper dotted lines). As will become clear later on, net migration assumptions are highly speculative at present.

2. THE DEMOGRAPHIC COMPONENT

The demographic component of the labour force potential follows the evolution of births. Figure 2 represents the evolution since the end of the Second World War. The baby boom during the sixties turned into a sharp decline in birth rates in the seventies and eighties. The recent upward trend at the end of the eighties does not indicate a new change in fertility, it is rather an echo effect of the baby boom during the sixties.

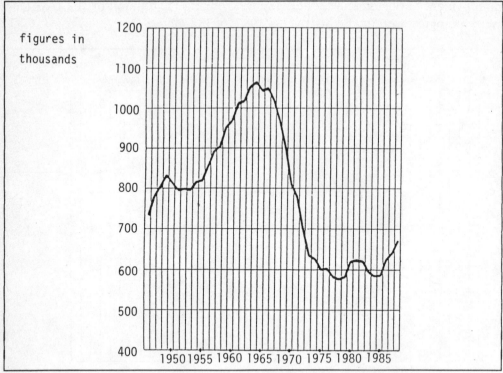

figures in
thousands

FIGURE 2:   Evolution of Births 1946 - 1988 (Statitisches Bundesamt)

On the labour market the influence of the baby boom is still prevailing. As can be seen in Fig. 1, the peak was reached in 1989. Although children of foreign workers still continued to increase the labour force potential, this effect was overcompensated by the decline in the demographic component of the German labour force potential in 1990.

Figure 3 represents the further development of the German labour force potential given alternative assumptions with regard to fertility rates. There are different models describing the effects of constant, increasing, and decreasing net repoduction rates. In any case, the demographic component of the German labour force potential will decline between 3.5 and 4.5 millions.

The most striking result is the impact on the age structure. Other things being equal, the age group 15 up to 30 will reduce its share in the German labour force potential from one-third in 1985 to one-fifth in 2000. At the same time the baby boom generation grows older entering the age group 30 up to 50 and reaching 55 per cent of the German labour force potential in 2000 (compare the dotted lines in Fig. 4). As a result company manpower planning and further training and re-training will gain importance.

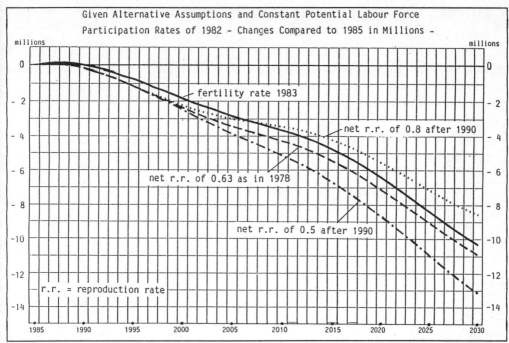

FIGURE 3:   Demographic Component of the German Labour Potential 1985 -
2030 (Klauder, 1986)

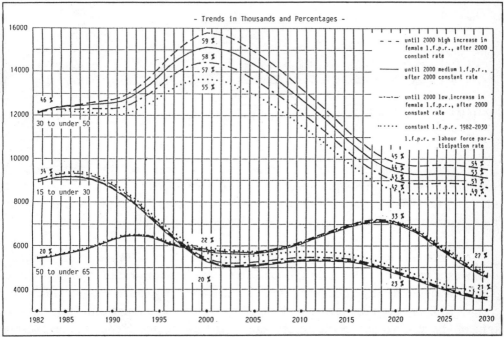

FIGURE 4:   Development of the German Labour Force Potential (Excluding
Foreigners) by Three Age-Groups, 1982 - 2030 (Klauder, 1988)

3. THE BEVAVIOURAL COMPONENT

The behavioural component reflects the change in age and sex-specific labour force participation rates because of (a) a higher female participation rate in the medium age group, (b) an increased participation and longer stay in higher education, and (c) earlier retirement.

(a) The impact of the increasing female labour force participation rate is shown in Figure 5.

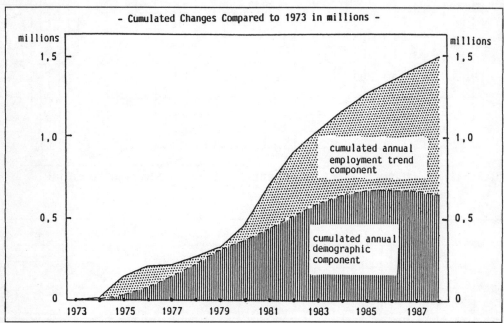

FIGURE 5:   German Female Labour Force Potential, 1973 - 1988 (Klauder, 1988)

In 1979 almost the whole increase was the result of the demographic component, which in 1988 merely counted for less than half of the total increase. In 1988 the behavioural component counted for about two-thirds of the 1.2 million rise in the femal labour force potential since 1979.

An international comparison of life-cycle patterns of female employment discloses a marked increase in labour force participation rates of medium age groups in all countries considered here. Figure 6 clearly shows the development in the FRG was even moderate compared to Denmark, France and Italy. In the light of the experience made in Denmark, the GDR and Sweden, the overall level of femal labour force participation in the FRG still leaves a margin.

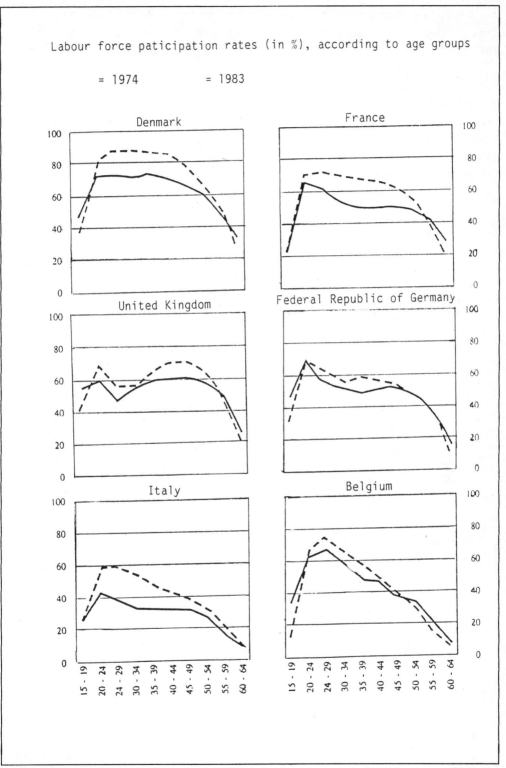

FIGURE 6: Life-cycle Patterns of Female Employment (Brinkmann, 1987)

58

Figure 6 also shows that during the ten years under consideration the labour force participation rates of younger and older age groups have decreased due to longer education and earlier retirement, respectively.

The increasing female labour force participation shown above is a long-term trend. Figure 7 reveals the behaviour of different age cohorts of married women and it makes clear that in nearly all cases (women without children, with one child, etc.) the labour force participation of younger cohorts is higher than that of older ones. The only exception are women with three or more children. Their share has continuously decreased during the last decades (see Figure 8).

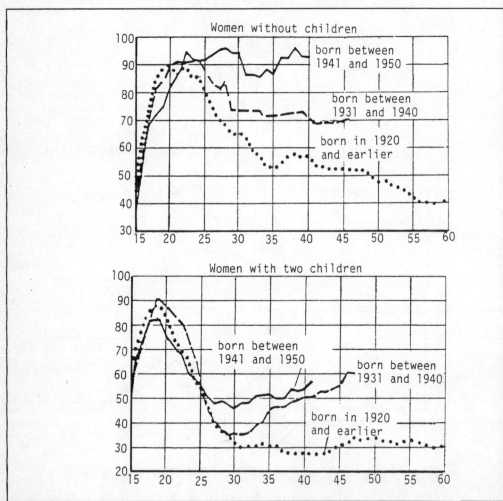

FIGURE 7   Labour Force Participation Rate of Married Women, by Specific Age-Groups (Percentage on total of the corresponding age-groups economically active during age indicated above) (The Socio-economic Panel, first year of inquiry 1984, calculations of the DIW)

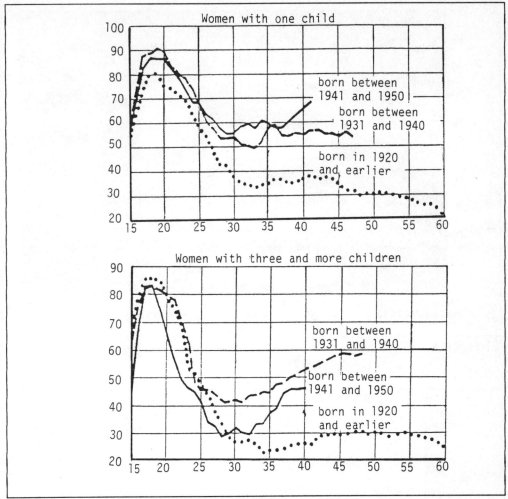

FIGURE 7   Labour Force Participation Rate of Married Women, by Specific Age-Groups

(b) The impact of changes in educational participation on age-specific labour force participation rates was indicated in Figure 6. Figure 9 represents the fundamental change in educational participation in the FRG during the last decades. While in 1960 only 28 per cent of all persons aged 18 years were in education including trainees and university students, this share boosted up to 78 per cent in 1985.

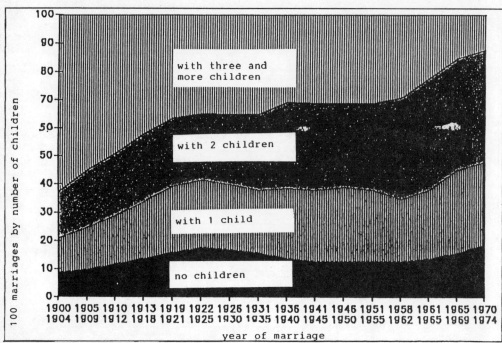

FIGURE 8: 100 Marriages During the Period 1900 - 1974, by Number of Live Births (Höhn, 1987)

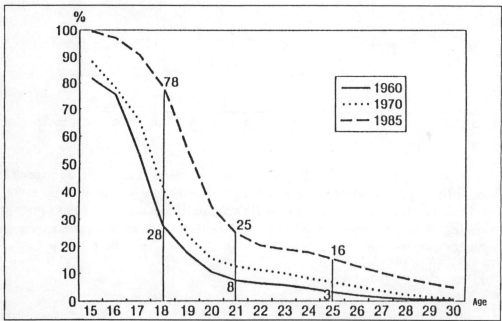

FIGURE 9: Educational Participation of the Population Aged 15 -30 years 1960, 1970, 1985 (Persons in education, including trainees and university students in per cent of the population of the same age) (IAB/BGR, educational accounting system)

The total behavioural (social) component of educational participation summed up to a labour supply withdrawal effect of about three million persons in 1985, which in times of continuous mass unemployment can be interpreted as an alleviating effect on the labour market.

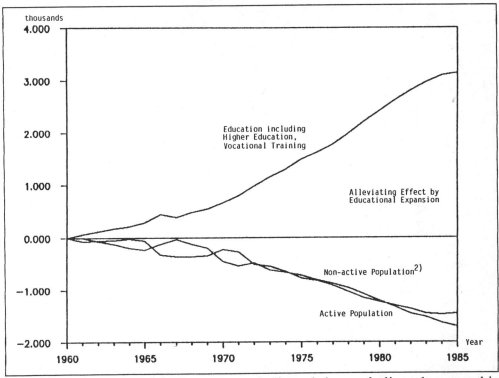

FIGURE 10: The Social Component (adjusted by excluding demographic trends) of the Development of the Education and Employment Systems, 1960 - 1985 (IAB/BGR, educational accounting system)

(c) Earlier retirement reduced age-specific labour force participation rates of older persons. Figure 11 clearly shows the effect of the introduction of a lower retirement age in the seventies on participation rates of persons aged between 60 and 64 as well as of the introduction of early retirement schemes on participation rates of persons aged between 55 and 59. As regards women aged between 55 and 59, the upward trend is a result of the overcompensating effect of an increasing age-specific propensity to enter the labour market as compared to the withdrawal effect of earlier retirement.

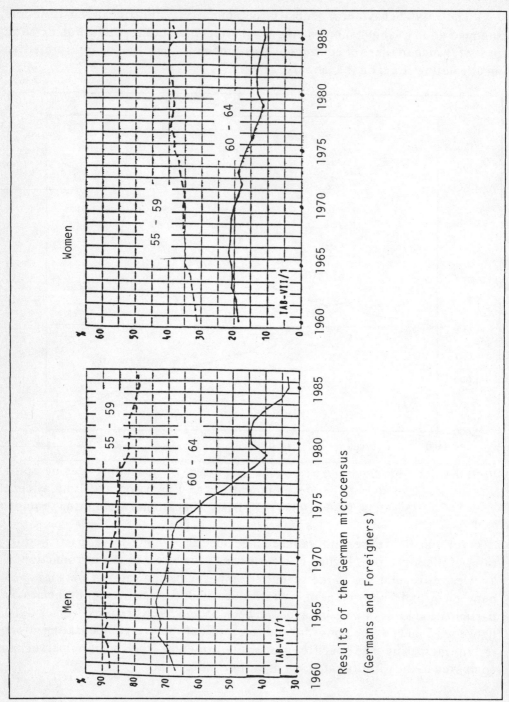

FIGURE 11: Labour Force Participation Rates of Man and Women Aged 55 - 59 and 60 - 64 (1960 - 1986) (Kühlewind, 1988)

4. THE MIGRATION COMPONENT

There are continuous streams of German and foreign migrants to and from the FRG resulting in changing patterns of net in- and out-migration. In the second half of the eighties both net results became increasingly positive. Figure 12 gives the results for the migration of foreigners.

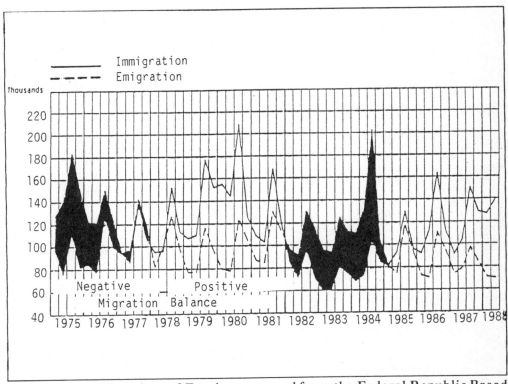

FIGURE 12: Migrations of Foreigners to and from the Federal Republic Based on Quarterly Figures from 1975 to 1988 - Immigrations, Emigrations, Migration, Balances - (Statistisches Bundesamt/IAB)

Additionally, immigration of Germans from East Block countries and from the GDR gains quantitative importance year after year. So, net migration in 1989 summed up to more than one million, two-thirds of this stream being net migration of Germans and one-third of foreigners. Although the 1989 figures are an exception and a result of specific historical events like the opening of the Iron Curtain, the corresponding movements will continue to be very important during the years to come. It is not possible, however, to predict them sufficiently accurately unde the pevailing circumstances. When we were to draw Figure 1 in 1989, we were not able to foresee the political changes in Eastern Europe. The net migration assumption of the upper dotted lines in Figure 1 therefore only represents some model calculations, the lower one of

		1987	1988	1989	1990	1991
		Annual change in thousands				
	1. Germans					
	1.1 Underlying long-term trends					
1	Demographic component	53	6	- 35	- 96	- 121
2	Enployment behaviour, medium variant	46	60	51	74	80
3	Total, medium variant	99	66	16	- 22	- 41
4	(For comparison:total higher variant)	(131)	(101)	(56)	(21)	(3)
5	1.2 Inflows of German migrants from East Bloc Countries and the GDR	38	62	160	504	341
6	1.3 Others	- 48	- 45	- 58	- 30	- 40
7	Total Germans	89	83	118	452	260
	2. Foreigners					
8	2.1 Demographic component excluding migrations (long-term trends)	47	44	46	45	40
9	2.2 Net migration excl. asylum seekers	15	41	94	75	40
10	2.3 Asylum seekers	35	40	32	30	31
11	Total foreigners	97	125	160	150	111
12	Total Germans and foreigners	186	208	278	602	371
13	For information: German migrants from East Bloc countries	78	203	377	350	300
14	German migrants from the GDR	19	40	344	350	175
15	Net migration Germans	77	192	671	650	425
16	Assumptions for the current years Net migration foreigners excl.asylum seekers	82	187	150	80	80
17	Asylum seekers	57	103	121	120	50

FIGURE 13: Calculation of the Labour Force Potential since 1987 (Joint Authorship 1989, own calculations)

which has become obsolete in the meanwhile. A more recent calculation of the migration component is presented in Figure 13, where the migration flows which habe been observed during the last three years and which are expected for 1990/91 have been transformed into additional potential labour force. This transformation considers legal constraints regarding the employment permit for residents from non-EC member states with special reference to asylum seekers, and the migrants' specific labour force participation rates.

Due to the selectivity of migration with regard to age groups and qualifications and due to the high female activity rate in the GDR, the expected labour force participation effect of 100 migrants from the GDR is 70. Assuming that the migration stream evenly spreads over the year, the net effect of - say- 350.000 migrants from the GDR in 1990 would lead to additional labour force of 125.00 persons on a yearly average and to an additional labour force of about 245.000 persons at the end of the year. Even higher flows are likely to happen.

Summing up, the increase in the labour force potential is now strongly influenced by the migration component.

In view of the completion of the European Internal Market, it is frequently argued that this will lead to additional net immigration. Similar expectations were expressed in the sixties as a result of the introduction of the principle of free movement of labour.

Other things being equal, we do not expect a dramatic change in internal migration patterns within the EC as a consequence of the united market. Migration is rather expected to be more selective in the case of highly skilled workers. The exchange of skilled personnel might increasingly be realized by work experience in multinational firms' establishments abroad. Given the fact that free movement of employees has already existed, the deregulation of obstacles to the freedom of establishment may lead to an increasing number of foreign self-employed persons migrating from one member state to another. Figure 14 shows the development of the number of foreign workers subject to social security in the FRG 1977 - 1987.

A widely unkown fact is the decreasing number of workers from EC member countries in the FRG during the last decade, the only exception being migrants from the UK and from Irelandas well as university graduates. The overall decline in the number of foreign workers from EC member countries is likely to be the result of decreasing pull- und push-factors stemming from international differences in job opportunities and welfare levels. These factors are not expected to change fundamentally during the next years

Nationality	Foreign Workers Total		EC		France		United Kingdom	
Vocational Qualification	1977	1987	1977	1987	1977	1987	1977	1987
Apprentices	29 558	53 227	13 300	11 881	701	233	781	697
Unskilled workers	1 293 023	997 467	524 308	315 597	24 087	20 072	11 429	14 324
Qualified workers, excluding higher education institutions	519 616	485 118	180 118	150 163	16 789	16 235	9 946	13 432
University graduates subject to social security	46 388	53 072	12 642	14 485	2 054	2 099	3 091	4 446
Employees subject to social security (total)	1 888 585	1 588 884	730 368	492 126	43 631	38 639	25 247	32 899

Nationality	Italy		Belgium		Netherlands		Luxembourg	
Vocational Qualification	1977	1987	1977	1987	1977	1987	1977	1987
Apprentices	4 384	1 901	339	68	1 484	322	56	16
Unskilled workers	212 892	127 748	3 952	2 759	14 144	7 606	379	267
Qualified workers, excluding higher education institutions	62 393	50 587	4 343	3 356	25 085	16 488	534	416
University graduates subject to social security	1 555	1 463	558	696	1 932	1 961	259	270
Employees subject to social security (total)	281 224	181 699	9 192	6 879	42 645	26 377	1 228	969

Nationality	Denmark		Ireland		Spain		Portugal	
Vocational Qualification	1977	1987	1977	1987	1977	1987	1977	1987
Apprentices	135	63	28	41	2 246	3 190	638	1 718
Unskilled workers	906	696	604	701	74 615	39 778	47 097	25 404
Qualified workers, excluding higher education institutions	1 694	1 365	432	575	22 706	20 193	12 250	8 409
University graduates subject to social security	330	283	106	176	744	888	175	271
Employees subject to social security (total)	3 065	2 407	1 170	1 493	100 311	64 049	60 160	35 802

Nationality	Greece	
Vocational Qualification	1977	1987
Apprentices	2 508	3 632
Unskilled workers	134 203	76 242
Qualified workers, excluding higher education institutions	23 946	19 107
University graduates subject to social security	1 838	1 932
Employees subject to social security (total)	162 495	100 913

FIGURE 14: Foreign Workes Subject ot Social Security in the Federal Republic of Germany by Nationality and Vocational Qualification, 1977 and 1987 (Walwei, 1989)

notwithstanding an internationally uneven distribution of the gains from the liberalization process. The trend towards additional migration of highly qualified labour may nevertheless continue.

5. AN EC LABOUR MARKET BALANCE

According to the basic structure underlying the presentation in Figure 1, the development of labour demand and supply within the EC member states is shown in Figure 15.

	Labour Force			Employment	Unemployment
	Demography	Labour Force Participation	Total		
1980–83	4,6	– 2,0	2,6	– 3,5	6,1
1984–86	2,9	0,7	3,6	1,7	1,9
1987–90	2,7	1,8	4,5	6,3	– 1,8
1980–90	10,2	0,5	10,7	4,5	6,2

FIGURE 15: EC Labour Market Balance 1980 - 1990 - Absolute Changes in Millions (Hofmann, 1989)

The demographic component is still important, but its influence is decreasing. Labour force participation leads to an increasing labour force. During the last three years the (expected) employment is growing faster than the labour force, resulting in a decrease in unemployment.

Forecasts of the population development and of the labour force in the EC member countries have recently been published by Prognos (Euro Report '89) and the European Commission (Employment in Europe 1989). The institute of Employment Research of the Federal Employment Services (IAB) is presently preparing a report on the development of labour market balances in the EC member countries under the regime of the united market, which will be published in 1990.

6. REFERENCES

Brinkmann, Ch. (1987), *Demographic Aspects of the Labour Force and Employment,* Council of Europe, Population Studies No. 19, p. 54

Höhn, Ch. (1987), *Soziale Konsequenzen eines Bevölkerungsrückgangs,* in: Zeitschrift für Bevölkerungswissenschaft, p. 291

Joint Authorship (1989), *Zur Arbeitsmarktentwicklung 1989/90,* in: Mitteilungen aus der Arbeitsmarkt- und Berufsforschung, 4/1989

Klauder, W. (1990), *Längerfristige Arbeitsmarktperspektiven,* in: Aus Politik und Zeitgeschichte, Beilage zur Wochenzeitung Das Parlament, B 3/90, p. 21

Klauder, W. (1986), *Auswirkungen der zukünftigen Bevölkerungsentwicklung auf den Arbeitsmarkt, Analysen auf der Grundlage von Modellrechnungen des Instituts für Arbeitsmarkt- und Berusforschung* (Vortrag auf der Hauptversammlung der Deutschen Statistischen Gesellschaft 1985), in: Allgemeines Statistisches Archiv, H. 1/1986, p. 75 - 96

Klauder, W. (1988), *Längerfristige Arbeitsmarktperspektiven für die Bundesrepublik Deutschland* (Vortrag in der Georg- von-Vollmar-Akademie, Kochel, am 8.1.1988, revised version in: Hesse, J.-J., Rolff, H.-G., Zöpel, Ch. (eds.) (188), Zukunftswissen und Bildungsperspektiven, Forum Zukunft Bd. 3, Baden-Baden

Kühlewind, G. (1988), *Age and Procedures of Retirement in Germany - Present Situation, Past Evolution and Forecast,* Working Paper presented at the International Seminar on the Aging of Population in Paris

o.V., *Immer mehr Frauen im Beruf,* DIW-Wochenbericht 29/87

Tessaring, M. et al. (1989), *Die Bildungsgesamtrechnung des Instituts für Arbeitsmarkt- und Berufsforschung,* Beiträge zur Arbeitsmarkt- und Berufsforschung, 126

Walwei, U. (1989), *Die soziale Dimension des Binnenmarktes,* Materialien aus der Arbeitsmarkt- und Berufsforschung, 8/1989

Hofmann, Cluas F. (1989), *The European Community's Economic and Employment Policy Strategy for the 90s,* Paper presented at the Conference of the European Association of Labour Economists in Turin, September 1989

POPULATION DEVELOPMENT IN GREECE
ACCORDING TO NEW DATA ON FERTILITY

George N. Tziafetas
Greek Productivity Center, Athens

1. POPULATION DEVELOPMENT DURING THE POST-WAR PERIOD

Greece, with its 9.8 million inhabitants, is a rather sparsely settled country (78 persons per km^2). Considering that the Athens and Thessaloniki areas have more than 4 million, the rest of the country has an average density of less than 44 persons per km^2.

The present distribution (Table 1.1) is a result of a quite short evolutionary process which began after the second world war (data after 1951) with the following characteristics:

a) High fertility rates at the beginning of the period, which has been gradually reduced, however, approaching the replacement level of 2.1 children per woman in 1981.

b) Strong population mobility towards the large urban centers of the country, mainly to Athens and Thessaloniki, mostly from the rural areas.

c) Low mortality rates, which had been continuously increased until 1981, because of the ageing of the population.

d) Greece was mainly a rural area, which, after a period of high fertility rates and strong emigration flow, moved, after 1981, into a new demographic era with continuously decreasing fertility rates below the replacement level.

Demographic statistical data in Greece are available from the National Statistical Service of Greece (NSSG). Thus, the results of the last censuses during the post - war period in 1951, 1961, 1971, and 1981 have been published providing estimates of the ageing of population. Table 1.2 illustrates the proportion of young (< 15) and elderly (> 64) people, the index of ageing (elderly population relative to young population) and the dependency ratio (young and elderly population relative to working - age population). As it seems from these data, a continuous increase in the proportion of elderly people is observed which creates a more rapid increase of the index of ageing.

It could be said that the ageing of population had been affected, until 1980, by the emigration towards the western European countries, mainly to West Germany.

The strong emigration flow, mainly from the rural areas in Greece, led to the phenomenon of a quite constant total fertility rate during the post-war period.

Emigration was the most important demographic component of population change in Greece, since it created a negative balance of 374.000 individuals of mainly young people aged under 40 years. First, it resulted in a negative emigration balance for Greece, but, after reaching a peak in the mid - 1960s, it declined irregularly until 1974.

Since then a slight net migration gain was noted due to return-migration and repatriation of Greeks from abroad. While the net population growth was below the level of natural increase throughout the post - war period up to 1974, it exceeded the rate of natural increase since then (Council of Europe, 1988).

In addition to external migration, the population distribution of Greece has been influenced by internal migration flows, with some rural areas experiencing significant levels of emigration and others, mainly urban centers, receiving large inflows of migrants. Table 1.1 reveals the whole process during the period 1961 - 80, where the Greater Athens Area has absorbed the main part of the real increase of the population.

Total fertility rate was fluctuating around 2.2 between 1960 and 1980 due to migration flow, while, after 1980, it continuously declined and reached 1.66 in 1985 which corresponds to a net reproduction rate of 0.77. Recent calculations with statistical data in 1988 estimate a value of 1.53 for the total fertility rate. It may be noted that total fertility rates in urban and rural areas converge to the same value (Table 1.4). Thus, due to the sharp fertility decline during the last 7 years, a rapid increase of population ageing is observed in an accelerating way.

Table 1.3 illustrates the life expectancy during the post - war period at the beginning of various ages. As it can be seen from these data, the gain of about 10 years in life expectancy was mainly in young ages, whereas it was very limited at other ages.

Thus, it may be said that it was a result of the rapid decline of the infant mortality rate.

Mortality is very low in all ages in Greece, while the age- and sex-specific rates decline further. Thus, the crude death rate, owing to the ageing of population, had gradually increased from 7.1 in the 1950s to 9.6 in 1987 per 1000 persons.

2. THE DEMOGRAPHIC PROJECTIONS

Although demographic projections are, of course, subject to considerable uncertainty, because both birth and mortality rates may change in unexpected ways, the age structure can be predicted with a reasonable degree of certainty up to the turn of this century. Beyond this time - point, the projections become, of course, increasingly less certain mainly due to unexpected changes in fertility rates. Nevertheless, a sharp increase in the proportion of elderly people from the early part of the next century is expected, even more in the case of an increase of the fertility rates at the replacement level.

In an explicit population projection the population structure may be considered according to the age of the population (cohort - component projection). Thus, the projection could be determined by the following formula:

$$P^{(r+1)} = (Z + M) P^{(r)} = G P^{(r)},$$

where :

Z: a $(w+w)$ sub - diagonal matrix where the elements of the sub - diagonal are the survivor rates $_x S_{x+1}$, $(x = 1, 2...., w-1)$, the elements of the first row are the rates b_x (some of these rates are zero) and all other elements are zero,

M: a (wxw) sub - diagonal matrix where the elements of the sub - diagonal are the rates m_x $(x = 1, 2,..., w-1)$,

$P^{(r)}$: a column vector where the elements are the population $P(x)^{(r)}$,

G : the growth operator,

$P(x)^{(r)}$: the population in the x - th age group at the time r $(x = 1, 2,...., w)$,

b_x : the number of births that survive to the end of a unit time interval per person, in the x - th child bearing age group,

$_xS_{x+1}$: the proportion of people in the x - th age group who survive to x + 1-th age group after the unit time interval,

m_x : the net migration rate for the x - th age group.

Such a model seems to be inapplicable in the case of Greece, because of the lack of statistical data about the migration process for each age group. Thus, it is more convenient to apply the above model by estimating the net migration rates having the results of the last censuses in 1971 and 1981 according to the following formula:

M_1 (net number of emigrants) = P(1981)-P(1971) . S_x
(Forward equation)

M_2 (net number of emigrants) = P(1981)/S_x-P(1971)
(Backward equation)

M (net number of emigrants) = $(M_1 + M_2)/2$,

where S_x is the survival rate during the time period 1971 - 1980.

According to the above equations, the net number of emigrants in each 5 - year age group has been determined in a vector form respectively for males and females and for each of the 10 geographical sub - regions in Greece. It may be noted that there is no substantial difference from the statistical data provided by the NSSG as aggregated results of the lost census in 1981.

In order to determine the parameter b_x it was necessary to compute the number of births in each sub - region according to the number of mothers in each age group. Thus, it was further necessary to estimate the population level at the middle of each year and take into consideration the survival rate during the first age interval.

Similarly, it was necessary to estimate the parameters $_xS_{x+1}$. For such an estimate of the first and last age intervals some appropriate formulae have been used in an approximate way.

3. THE RESULTS OF THE PROJECTIONS

Referring to the previous paragraph the following four scenarios are considered:

a) closed population and total fertility rate at the level of 1981,
b) closed population and total fertility rate at the level of 1985,
c) closed population and total fertility rate at the level of 1988.
d) open population and total fertility rate at the level of 1985.

The assumption of constant mortality at the level of 1981 does not diverge very much from reality, insofar it has already reached a very good level. The further reduction of the infant mortality rate would not substantially affect the total population development as it would be balanced by the expected small increase of deaths in the working - age intervals (Table 3.1).

A question remains open concerning the evolution of emigration over time, as there exist serious factors affecting it. At first, the integration of the accession of Greece to E.E.C. creates the suspicion of a new commencement of external migration to the E.E.C. countries after 1988, as it has been already mentioned by the Intergovernmental Committee for Migration (ICM).

On the other hand, the financing of the Mediterranean Intergrated Programs (IMP) would strengthen the regional development and would restrain the tendency for emigration from the frontier and rural areas. Thus, it is finally assumed in model D that the migration rate would be half of the value observed during the foregoing decade 1971 - 1980 in all regions (Table 3.2).

A normal consequence of the fertility decline will be the total population reduction as it can be seen in Table 3.3 (scenarios A,B,D) and in Figures 1 and 2. In addition to the general conclusion, the crucial result of the expected population change will be the fast increase of the population ageing in all regions in Greece.

The process is more accelerating in some rural regions (Ionian and Aegean Islands, Epirus, etc.), in comparison to the total population. Moreover, the migratory factor enforces the evolution of the ageing process in some rural areas, where untill now an internal migration towards the urban centers was observed.

As it can be seen in Table 3.4, the proportion of elderly females on th Ionian Islands will differ in 2050 between scenarios A and B by approximately 30%, while the decrease in the proportion of the young males and females will be about the same. It may be noted that the differences between the scenarios A and B give a measure of the influence of the fertility decline on the changes of the population distribution, since the total fertility rate in 1981 in Greece was at the replacement level (2.09 children per woman aged between 15 and 49 years).

The proportion of young people in the population is projected to fall quite sharply after 2000 as the assumed low fertility begins to affect birth rates. Thus for example on the Ionian Islands the proportion of males will decrease from 22% in 1985 to 18% in 2010 and to 15% in 2050 (scenario B).

Finally, it may be noted that population ageing has important implications on the size and age structure on the working population. In comparison to the rapid growth in the numbers of the working - age people during the period 1950 - 70, as a result of large cohorts born immediately after World War II, the proportion of this people remained quite constant after 1971 and will remain constant up to the end of this century. In about 20 years some geographical regions are expected to show a continuous decrease in the absolute number of working - age people. By the decade 2021 - 30, the numbers of working - age people are projected to fall in almost all regions, when the impact of low fertility rates on the numbers of entrants will be compounded by the exit of large cohorts from the working - age group to the elderly age group.

The most crucial point of the evolutionary process might be the changes on the structure of the working population. Figure 3 reveals the whole process, where a shift of the mean age of the working population is observed.

It may be noted that the proportion of working population aged under 40 years will be 41.2% (= 1.478.000 persons, scenario B) or 40.8% (= 1.394.000 persons, scenario C), while it was 50.2% (= 1.775.000 persons) in 1981.

The demographic changes mentioned in the foregoing paragraph, will affect, of course, the general economy, employment and in the future the labour market. A range of social policies related to education, health care, pension provisions, family and child support will also be affected by the sharp increase of population ageing. A crude index to measure the impact of the demographic changes on the social support burden is the dependency ratio of the number of the young and elderly persons (x100) relative to working - age persons. Table 3.5 illustrates estimates of the total dependency ratio in some OECD countries. In comparison to OECD projections (medium fertility variant of 1983), the projections with lower fertility rates (scenario B and C) show a further increase particularly during the period 2011 - 1050 (figure 5).

Because of the population ageing, an important divergence between the young and elderly people dependency ratio is observed. The elderly people will comprise an increasing proportion of the dependency in the coming decades, while the proportion of young dependants is expected to decline. Thus, in 1980, an average of 40% of those in the dependent age groups in Greece were elderly persons, while in 2050, thcy have been projected (scenarios B and C) to be over 70%. Comparing Figure 5a with Figures 5b and 5c a shift of more than 15 years is observed regarding the intersection of the curves which represent the young and elderly dependency ratio.

The social policy implications of such an evolutionary process are more important in Greece, particularly to the social expenditure, because public health care programs are primarily directed towards the elderly, with the remainder of the population relying heavily on private provisions. As a result, it can be said that an extremely sharp increase of social expenditure is expected in Greece which could be strengthened by the re-organisation of health care programmes.

4.   REFERENCES

Council of Europe, *Recent demographic developments in the member States of the Council of Europe*, 1988.

National Statistical Service of Greece, *Statistical Yearbooks* and *Monthly Statistical Bulletin*, after 1972.

OECD, *Ageing populations - The social policy implications*, 1988.

Tziafetas G. and J. Tzougas, *Regional Population Projections in Greece* (in Greek with an extended summary in French), Proccedings of the Franco - Hellenique Demographic Conference held in Athens, May 17 - 21, 1987.

United Nations, *Population projections - Methodology of the UN*, E83, XIII 7.1985.

Valaoras Vs., *The Population of Greece during the second half of the 20th century*, edition of NSSG, Athens 1980.

Willekens F. and A. Rogers, *Spatial Population Analysis : Methods and Computer Programmes*, RR - 78 - 18, IIASA, 1978.

5. FIGURES AND TABLES

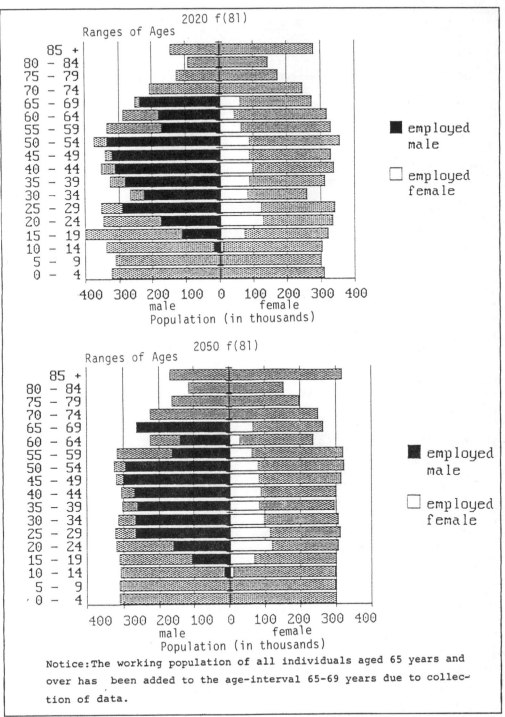

FIGURE 1: Distribution of Total Population and Working Population in Greece (Scenario A)

78

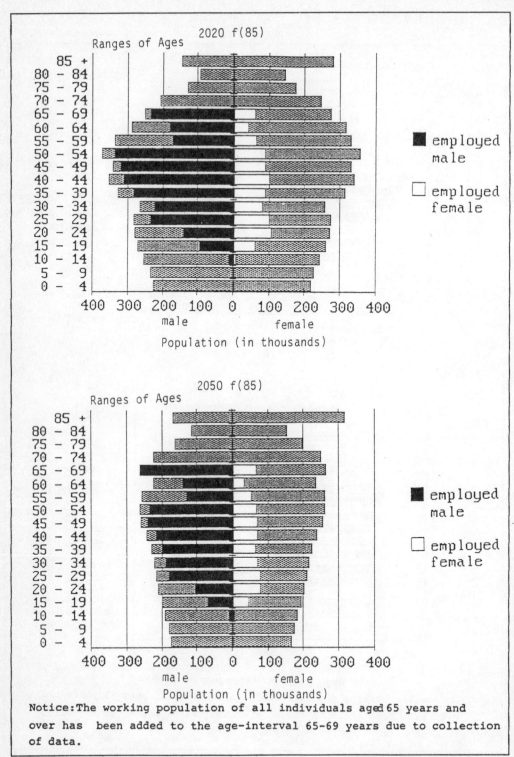

FIGURE 2: Distribution of Total Population and Working Population in Greece (Scenario B)

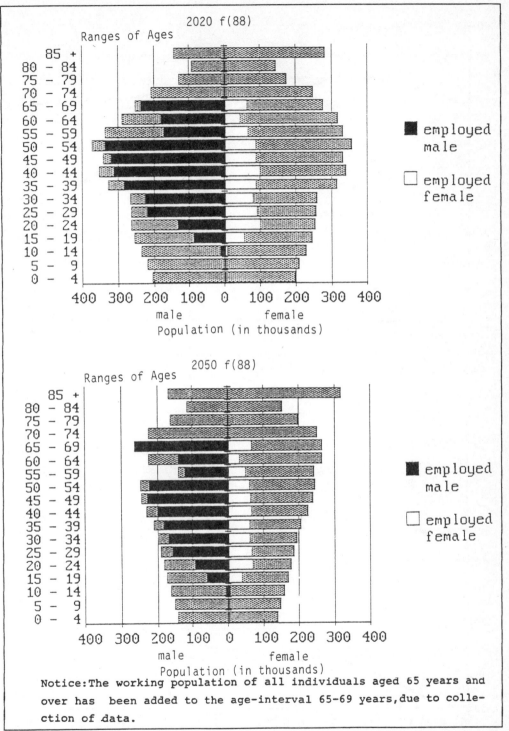

FIGURE 3: Distribution of Total Population and Working Population in Greece (Scenario C)

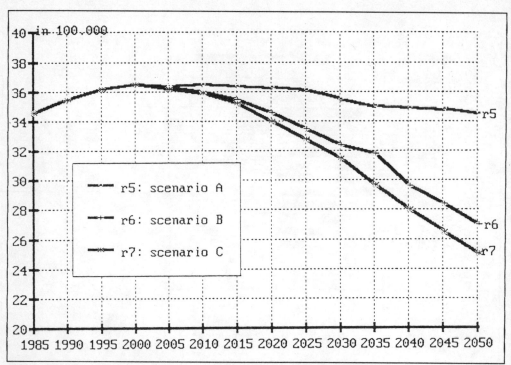

FIGURE 4: Economically Active Population of Greece

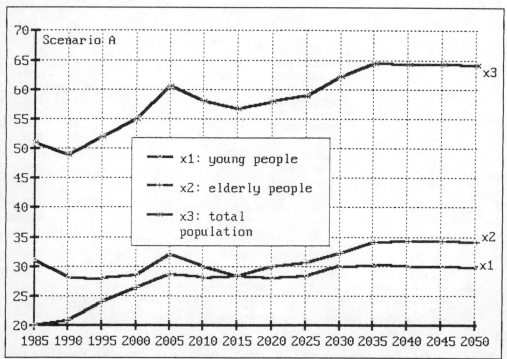

FIGURE 5a: Evolution of the Dependency Ratio   (Scenario A)

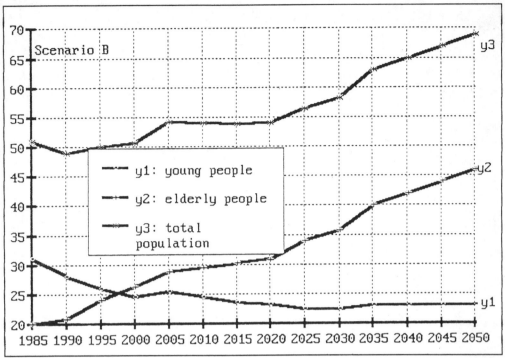

FIGURE 5b: Evolution of the Dependency Ratio   (Scenario B)

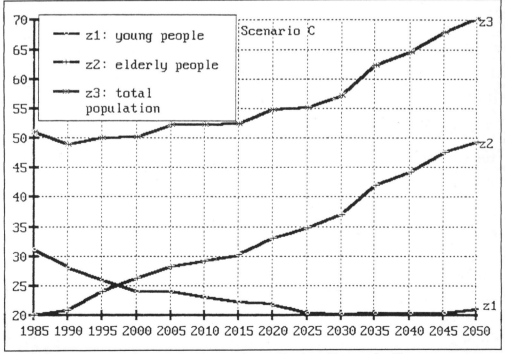

FIGURE 5c: Evolution of the Dependency Ratio   (Scenario C)

82

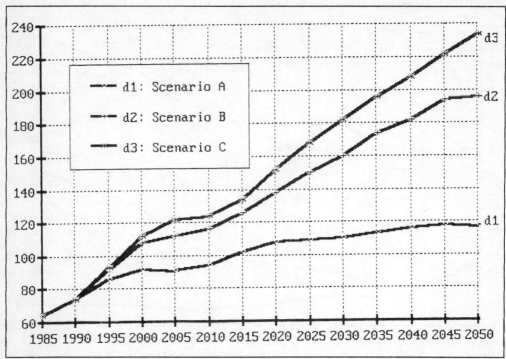

FIGURE 6: Evolution of the Ageing Index in Greece

Region	Population (x 103)			Changes (%)		Rates*	
	1961	1971	1981	1961 - 70	1971 - 80	Birth	Death
Greater Athens	1852.7	2540.2	3027.3	37.1	19.2	20.4	9.2
Rest of C.Greece	970.9	992.2	1099.5	2.2	10.8	16.7	9.9
Peloponnesos	1096.3	986.9	1012.5	-10.0	2.6	15.7	11.2
Ionian Islands	212.5	184.4	182.6	-13.2	-1.0	14.4	13.5
Epirus	352.6	310.3	324.5	-12.0	4.6	16.6	9.3
Thessaly	689.9	659.9	695.6	- 4.4	5.4	17.7	9.3
Macedonia	1896.1	1890.6	2121.9	- 0.3	12.2	17.5	9.4
Thrace	356.5	329.5	345.2	- 7.6	4.7	18.0	10.0
Aegean Islands	477.4	417.8	428.5	-12.5	2.6	15.4	12.3
Crete	483.2	456.6	502.1	- 5.5	10.0	18.1	10.0

*Average crude rates during the decades 1971 - 80.
 Source:National Statistical Service of Greece (NSSG).

TABLE 1.1: Population Development in Greece

Age - Inter	1951 urban	rural	1961 urban	rural	1971 urban	rural	1981 urban	rural	1985 total
<15	23.3	32.3	22.2	29.7	23.1	26.8	23.4	22.7	20.9
15-64	70.7	60.4	71.0	61.3	67.8	60.3	66.2	60.0	65.7
>64	6.0	7.3	6.8	9.0	9.1	12.9	10.4	17.3	13.4
Index of ageing	25.8	22.6	30.6	30.3	39.4	48.1	44.4	76.2	64.1
Dependency ratio	41.4	65.6	40.8	63.1	47.5	65.8	51.1	66.7	52.2

Source: Census Results, NSSG.

TABLE 1.2: The Population Distribution in Large Age Intervals, the Index of Ageing and the Dependency Ratio in Urban and Rural Regions in Greece

Age (years)	Males 1950	1960	1970	1980	Females 1950	1960	1970	1980
0	63.4	67.3	70.1	72.1	66.6	70.4	73.6	76.6
1	66.8	70.3	72.1	72.8	69.8	73.2	75.3	77.0
5	64.1	67.2	68.7	69.0	67.1	70.0	71.7	73.2
20	50.2	52.7	54.1	54.5	53.0	55.5	57.1	58.4
40	32.3	34.0	35.1	35.6	34.8	36.4	37.8	38.9
50	23.7	25.0	25.9	26.4	26.1	27.1	28.3	29.5
60	16.2	16.9	17.5	18.2	18.0	18.6	19.3	20.6
70	10.1	10.3	10.6	11.5	11.1	11.6	11.7	13.2
80	5.4	5.6	5.8	6.7	5.9	6.2	6.2	7.6

Sources: MSSG.

TABLE 1.3: Life Expectancy at the Beginning of Different Ages

Age - Int	1960 Total	Urban	Rural	1970 Total	Urban	Rural
< 20	27.4	23.5	27.1	36.9	34.1	40.2
20 - 24	109.7	81.7	121.2	140.9	126.8	162.5
25 - 29	157.5	125.5	152.5	143.0	131.3	160.7
30 - 34	105.7	80.9	102.9	93.7	86.5	103.9
35 - 39	48.6	33.8	43.4	42.6	39.9	45.8
40 - 44	14.4	7.4	10.8	9.1	7.6	10.8
> 44	2.0	0.8	1.7	1.2	0.9	1.6
TFR	2.27	1.72	2.30	2.34	2.14	2.63

Age - Int	1980 Total	Urban	Rural	1983* Total	Urban	Rural
< 20	50.5	47.4	61.2	43.7	40.5	55.3
20 - 24	157.7	142.9	170.6	139.7	124.5	150.0
25 - 29	134.3	133.3	121.3	116.5	124.5	112.6
30 - 34	75.7	71.4	56.9	59.4	64.1	46.1
35 - 39	26.5	29.3	23.8	23.0	30.2	19.1
40 - 44	6.7	6.7	6.5	5.0	5.6	3.7
> 44	0.8	0.9	0.8	0.6	0.6	0.5
TFR	2.18	2.16	2.21	1.94	1.95	1.94

*Estimates.

Source: Calculations with data from National Statistical Service
of Greece.

TABLE 1.4: Fertility Rates in Greece

Age Intervals	Males	Females
Sγ	0.9774	0.9918
0 – 4	0.9963	0.9969
5 – 9	0.9981	0.9987
10 – 14	0.9970	0.9985
15 – 19	0.9955	0.9981
20 – 24	0.9947	0.9978
25 – 29	0.9940	0.9974
30 – 34	0.9929	0.9968
35 – 39	0.9907	0.9953
40 – 44	0.9864	0.9923
45 – 49	0.9772	0.9865
50 – 54	0.9603	0.9761
55 – 59	0.9329	0.9571
60 – 64	0.8909	0.9250
65 – 69	0.8295	0.8755
70 – 74	0.7457	0.8023
75 – 79	0.6386	0.7013
80 – 84	0.6223	0.6957

TABLE 3.1: The Survival Probability in Greece

Age Intervals	Male	Female
0 – 4	16.017	15.116
5 – 9	14.174	14.155
10 – 14	– 480	– 83
15 – 19	1937	3.868
20 – 24	-7.181	1.808
25 – 29	-2.240	3.113
30 – 34	-1.494	12.739
35 – 39	15.116	12.444
40 – 44	18.302	13.095
45 – 49	11.689	2.579
50 – 54	8.731	3.466
55 – 59	3.159	1.645
60 – 64	2.118	109
65 – 69	1.928	2.965
70 – 74	916	2.096
75 – 79	– 590	– 820
80 – 84	– 637	-2.840
85 +	2.274	5.410

TABLE 3.2: The Net Migration Vector in Greece (the elements of the vector have a value of the half of the migration flow during the decade 1971 - 1980)

		Gr.Athens	Rest of C.G	Pelo/sos	Ionian Isl.	Epirus
1	1985	3124	1125	1030	182	332
2	1990	3212	1158	1056	183	344
3	1995	3275	1192	1082	184	355
4	2000	3320	1223	1106	184	365
5	2005	3348	1246	1125	184	373
6	2010	3359	1261	1140	184	379
7	2015	3356	1275	1156	184	386
8	2020	3342	1290	1176	184	393
9	2025	3317	1306	1197	185	401
10	2030	3281	1319	1216	186	408
11	2035	3239	1328	1234	186	414
12	2040	3192	1335	1250	186	420
13	2045	3143	1339	1264	186	426
14	2050	3093	1341	1277	185	431

		Thessaly	Macedonia	Thrace	Aegean Isl.	Crete
1	1985	714	2178	356	435	517
2	1990	738	2248	369	441	535
3	1995	763	2311	382	449	554
4	2000	785	2363	394	457	573
5	2005	804	2398	404	463	589
6	2010	818	2416	412	469	604
7	2015	833	2428	420	475	620
8	2020	849	2440	429	481	636
9	2025	867	2450	437	488	654
10	2030	884	2454	445	493	670
11	2035	901	2450	452	498	687
12	2040	917	2440	458	502	703
13	2045	934	2426	465	507	717
14	2050	949	2410	472	510	734

TABLE 3.3a: Population Development in Greece (x1000, Sencario A)

		Gr. Athens	Rest of C.G.	Pelo/sos	Ionian Isl.	Epirus
1	1985	3124	1125	1030	182	332
2	1990	3171	1141	1040	181	337
3	1995	3195	1156	1050	180	340
4	2000	3203	1169	1058	179	343
5	2005	3192	1174	1060	177	343
6	2010	3158	1169	1056	174	341
7	2015	3102	1157	1049	171	337
8	2020	3029	1143	1040	168	332
9	2025	2942	1128	1032	166	327
10	2030	2844	1109	1021	163	321
11	2035	2736	1086	1006	160	313
12	2040	2621	1057	987	156	304
13	2045	2502	1023	963	152	293
14	2050	2381	986	936	147	282

		Thessaly	Macedonia	Thrace	Aegean Isl.	Crete
1	1985	714	2178	356	435	517
2	1990	727	2210	363	438	526
3	1995	739	2235	370	441	536
4	2000	749	2249	375	445	545
5	2005	755	2245	379	448	551
6	2010	755	2220	379	448	554
7	2015	751	2179	377	448	555
8	2020	745	2132	374	447	555
9	2025	740	2079	370	447	554
10	2030	733	2019	365	445	551
11	2035	724	1949	358	441	547
12	2040	712	1868	349	436	540
13	2045	698	1782	340	431	532
14	2050	682	1691	331	424	521

TABLE 3.3b: Population Development in Greece (x1000, Scenario B)

		Gr.Athens	Rest of C.G.	Pelo/sos	Ionian Isl.	Epirus
1	1985	3243	1146	1024	181	330
2	1990	3290	1160	1033	180	334
3	1995	3332	1173	1038	177	336
4	2000	3349	1185	1043	175	338
5	2005	3340	1191	1046	174	338
6	2010	3304	1187	1043	171	336
7	2015	3246	1175	1035	168	331
8	2020	3172	1160	1025	165	325
9	2025	3084	1144	1016	162	319
10	2030	2979	1126	1005	159	313
11	2035	2861	1103	991	156	306
12	2040	2734	1075	975	152	299
13	2045	2602	1043	954	149	290
14	2050	2472	1007	930	144	279

		Thessaly	Macedonia	Thrace	Aegean Isl.	Crete
1	1985	708	2228	352	434	523
2	1990	720	2259	359	437	532
3	1995	730	2284	364	439	541
4	2000	739	2300	369	442	549
5	2005	745	2299	372	445	556
6	2010	746	2274	372	447	559
7	2015	742	2233	370	447	560
8	2020	736	2184	367	446	559
9	2025	730	2130	363	444	558
10	2030	723	2070	358	442	555
11	2035	715	2000	351	439	551
12	2040	705	1920	343	434	545
13	2045	693	1833	335	430	537
14	2050	678	1741	325	424	527

TABLE 3.3c: Population Development in Greece (x1000, Scenario C)

Regions	Age interv.	1985A		2010A		2050A		1985B		2010B		2050B	
		M	F	M	F	M	F	M	F	M	F	M	F
Greater	0 - 14	23	20	19	17	18	16	23	20	16	14	13	12
Athens Area	15 - 64	67	67	66	63	63	59	67	67	68	65	62	56
	65 +	10	13	15	20	19	25	10	13	16	21	25	32
Rest of	0 - 14	23	22	21	20	20	18	23	22	18	16	14	13
Central	15 - 64	64	63	64	60	62	59	64	63	66	62	61	56
Greece	65 +	13	15	15	20	18	23	13	15	16	22	25	31
Peloponnesos	0 - 14	22	21	21	20	21	19	22	21	18	17	15	14
	15 - 64	63	61	62	60	61	60	63	61	64	61	60	57
	65 +	15	18	17	20	18	21	15	18	18	22	25	29
Ionian Isl.	0 - 14	22	19	21	19	19	18	22	19	18	16	15	14
	15 - 64	61	60	62	60	63	60	61	60	64	62	62	58
	65 +	17	21	17	21	18	22	17	21	18	22	23	28
Epirus	0 - 14	23	21	22	20	21	19	23	21	18	16	14	12
	15 - 64	64	62	63	59	63	59	64	62	66	61	61	55
	65+	13	17	15	21	16	22	13	17	16	23	25	33
Thessaly	0 - 14	23	22	23	21	22	20	23	22	20	17	17	15
	15 - 64	65	63	62	59	63	60	65	63	64	61	63	57
	65+	12	15	15	20	15	20	12	15	16	22	20	28
Macedonien	0 - 14	23	21	20	19	19	18	23	21	16	15	13	12
	15 - 64	67	66	65	61	63	60	67	66	67	64	61	56
	65 +	10	13	15	20	18	22	10	13	17	21	26	32
Thrace	0 - 14	23	23	22	21	22	21	23	23	18	17	16	15
	15 - 64	68	64	65	61	63	60	68	64	68	63	62	59
	65 +	9	13	13	18	15	19	9	13	14	20	22	26
Aegean Isl.	0 - 14	22	21	21	20	20	19	22	21	19	18	17	16
	15 - 64	62	60	64	60	62	60	62	60	65	62	62	59
	65 +	16	19	15	20	18	21	16	19	16	20	21	25
Crete	0 - 14	25	22	23	21	22	21	25	22	19	18	16	15
	15 - 64	61	61	62	60	61	60	61	61	64	62	60	58
	65 +	14	17	15	19	17	19	14	17	17	20	24	27

TABLE 3.4: Population Destributions (%) in 10 Geographical Regions in Greece

Total dependency ratio in some O.E.C.D countries

	1980	1990	2000	2010	2020	2030	1040	2050	changes % 1980-40	2010-50
France(1)	56.8	51.8	52.6	50.8	57.3	64.4	68.3	68.2	42	47
Germany(1)	50.8	44.0	48.3	50.5	54.3	68.7	64.8	69.9	47	48
Japan (1)	48.4	48.2	48.6	58.6	60.6	59.5	66.8	65.7	38	14
Spain (1)	58.1	52.2	51.9	47.8	49.0	58.4	68.4	69.0	18	43
Turkey(1)	78.1	65.9	59.1	49.0	47.3	54.3	56.7	51.9	-27	16
Greece(1)	56.1	48.3	51.3	53.3	54.1	58.0	61.9	62.6	10	16
Greece(2)	56.1	52.7	59.6	58.0	58.1	60.6	62.9	61.9	12	7
Greece(3)	56.1	50.4	52.6	52.3	53.3	57.4	64.0	67.3	14	29
Greece(4)	56.1	49.3	51.9	52.4	53.5	58.8	63.4	68.8	13	29

Source: (1) OECD projections 1988.
       (2) Scenario A.
       (3) Scenario B.
       (4) Scenario C.

TABLE 3.5:   Total Dependency Ratio in Some OECD Countries

TECHNOLOGICAL CHANGE IN MANUFACTURING: RESPONSES OF PERSONNEL MANAGEMENT IN A SPATIAL PERSPECTIVE

Sake Wagenaar
Egbert Wever
Department of Economic Geography
University of Nijmegen

1. INTRODUCTION

Technological change influences the spatial structure of economies in various ways. In this paper, the role of changing production technology in the manufacturing sector is discussed in relation to regional labour markets. This relationship between technology and labour market is two-sided. First, (regional) labour supply, especially from a qualitative point of view, can be seen as a constraint on technological change. Secondly, changing technology has consequences for the (regional) demand for labour. In reality, both relationships are closely intertwined, both qualitatively and quantitatively. An attempt is made to work out the second line of thought. Changing production technology can affect both the amount and the quality of labour demand. In this paper, attention is focused on this quality aspect.

2. TECHNOLOGY, ORGANIZATION AND COMPETITION

However, before dealing with technology and labour demand in detail, it must be stressed that regional labour markets are not only affected by technological change, but by many other trends as well. The following examples illustrate this.

First, it is known that many transnational companies, for example Philips, aim at reducing employment at their head-offices: a 'leaner and meaner' organization. The result is decentralization of employment in administration, R&D and management functions towards the main production centres. As a result, the sharp contrast between highly skilled jobs at the head quarters and the lower skilled jobs at the production plants will diminish.

The second remark refers to the 'back-to-basics' strategy which is very popular nowadays. For assembly activities this often implies a growing importance of subcontractors and co-makers. Because of 'zero-stock', 'just-in-time' and 'zero- faults' principles, large firms are trying to select the best subcontractors they can find. Between 1983 and 1989 the Dutch Rank Xerox plant reduced the number of subcontractors from 1200 to 150. The remaining subcontractors are vital for the successful operation of the assembly plant. As a result, proximity between subcontractors and their subcontracting firm becomes more important, and therefore the spatial pattern of subcontractors and their employees will change.

The third example relates to the central theme of this volume. In the future, the number of persons looking for jobs will diminish. At the same time, these people will be more highly educated. This higher education is expected to be accompanied by higher demands on the organization of work. An organization of work in which the capacities of employees are more fully utilized, stimulates their motivation, and increases their productivity. The new motor car factory of Volvo, located at Uddevalla, is an example of this trend (Alvstam, Ellegard, forthcoming). Although there are many non-technical factors affecting the quality and spatial distribution of jobs, no doubt, technology is important as well. The growing use of flexible production technologies is strongly related to changes in the environment in which firms operate. International competition has become more intense and its fundament has shifted from price to non-price factors. As markets are becoming more fragmented and unpredictable, firms are pressed to direct their competitive strategies more and more towards high quality, product differentiation and product innovation. In general, this shift in strategy cannot be successful with the usual labour organization and techniques (Cooke 1988; Scott, Cooke 1988; Schoenberger 1988).

The introduction of new technologies is often accompanied by organizational change, and organizational factors are very important for the success or failure of the introduction of new technologies. Technology is related to the division of labour within the firm at three levels: the division of tasks between man and machine, the division of tasks between the various occupations and functional levels within departments, and the division of tasks between departments (Alders, Christis 1988). Together, these three levels determine the content of jobs, and the qualifications required for these jobs.

As a result of economic and technological change, new methods of production are emerging, which may strongly affect the division of labour, not only within, but also between firms. In these 'new production conceptions' (as they have been called by Kern, Schumann), much attention is given to organizational and social factors, as the following quotation illustrates:

> *"Until now, rationalisation has pursued the Tayloristic principle of increasing labour division followed by a minimisation of human labour. Yet important potential productivity is wasted by applying these principles today. For this reason, (...) the management is trying to develop productivity by using human labour more efficient by integrating tasks and foster qualifications"* (Fuchs, Schamp, forthcoming).

The primacy of the technological factor is also challenged in practice, for example at the new Volvo plant in Uddevalla (Alvstam, Ellegard, forthcoming). In this new plant the human factor is assigned the principal part because of a number of motives:

1. the high rate of labour turnover in traditionally organized motor car factories and the great number of injuries in factories with repetitive work tasks;

2. the competition among employers for the youngsters, in anticipation of the decreasing size of the youth cohorts in the near future. As the level of education of these youngsters has increased, the would-be recruits will not be satisfied with the kind of work the automobile industry traditionally offers.

3. the low status of industrial jobs in Sweden nowadays. People prefer work in the service sector and in more glamorous jobs.

In response to these problems, Volvo established a new plant, characterized by small autonomous groups of (ten) workers producing a complete car. In order to make this possible, an electronic information system has been developed to make sure that components and material arrive at the assembly site at the right time and in the right order. This way of production requires each worker to master nearly all the tasks needed to produce a complete car. Besides traditional assembly tasks, the new jobs include checking components and materials, quality control and making adjustments.

In the new factory, ordinary blue-collar tasks will be combined with tasks usually handled by the white-collar staff. The working groups will plan some of their own tasks, on a daily or weekly basis, and group members will be involved in activities like budgeting and recruitment. By removing the sharp distinction between blue and white-collar jobs, Volvo makes industrial jobs more attractive for young, well-educated people.

So, the view of technology as the driving force behind changes in the labour process and the organization does not fit in with the new ideas on work methods emerging from the example given above. Changes in both the amount and quality of labour demand are to a great extent affected by decisions about the organization of the production process. The importance of technology in this respect is often overstated (In 't Veld 1981, Fruytier 1989).

3. TECHNOLOGICAL CHANGE AND LABOUR DEMAND

How is labour demand developing as a result of both organizational and technological changes? According to Kaplinsky (1987) there is little unanimity about the quantitative development of employment in connection with the rapid diffusion of micro-electronics. The results are very sensitive for the level of analysis (establishment, enterprise, sector, country, region), because technological change will usually entail changing divisions of labour, both within and between firms (e.g. subcontracting).

The relation between technological change and the qualitative aspects of labour demand may be examined at different levels and by different methods. Studies on the branch-level are often problematic because they conceal more than they reveal (e.g. Bekkering, Cramer, Oud 1988). Therefore, some examples on the firm-level will be given.

In a study about the introduction of computer-aided design (CAD) in the Standard Elektrik Lorenz company (SEL), Fuchs, Schamp (forthcoming) make a distinction between immediate and indirect impacts on labour. With immediate effects they allude to the quality of work in development and design. For the period between 1960 and 1988 they found that:

> "(...) there was a significant relative and absolute decrease in the number of semi-skilled workers and qualified personnel working in the design of printed circuit boards, the engineering design and the design of electronic circuits" (Fuchs, Schamp, forthcoming).

The number of industrial engineers underwent a contrasting development:

> "There was an increase in the relative and absolute number of industrial engineers (with university degrees) who design

printed circuit boards; in engineering design, only their relative number increased. Only in the design of electronic circuits, which was diminished to half the number of its former employees, did the number of industrial engineers decline absolutely (...). With no exception, only industrial engineers are working on the development of software, and their number has risen ten-fold in this period" (Fuchs, Schamp, forthcoming).

The indirect effects are difficult to measure, not only because they appear with a time lag, but also because many other factors may affect the labour profile of a department (e.g. globalization, subcontracting, back-to-basics). As the integration between CAD and CAM proceeds, the indirect effects will increase. The labour effects are most apparent in the secondary segment of the labour market. In this segment, standardization and redistribution of tasks occurs, while the number of jobs is reduced. The way the organization has been adapted is more important in explaining these effects than the new technology in itself. The organizational and technological changes not only affect workers with lower qualifications; the qualified personnel has been confronted with changes as well:

"On the shop floor, the foremen need more comprehensive knowledge of data processing than before, as does the personnel who set up machines; in addition their knowledge needs to apply to checking for and repairing defects. The production engineers' knowledge of machines may decrease, whereas their critical use of electronic data as well as their overall view of the entire production process must increase" (Fuchs, Schamp, forthcoming).

In the Netherlands, TNO has examined the effects of computer-aided manufacturing on job structure, selection criteria and recruitment strategies. One of the branches studied is the Dutch engineering industry, a branch in which replacement of conventional 'fixed purpose' metal working machines by more flexible CNC-machines ('Computer Numerical Control') can be observed. The study concentrates on the tasks assigned to operators of conventional machinery on one hand, and operators of computer controlled machinery on the other hand (Alders, Christis 1988).

Almost all operators of conventional machines carry out an integrated set of tasks: a mix of preparatory, operative and supportive tasks. For most of the operators of CNC-machines the mix of tasks is quite different. Three job structures have been observed:

1.   In forty-nine percent of the cases, the operators of CNC-machines both operate the machine, and make, test and correct the programs controlling the operations.

2.   In twenty-four percent of the cases these tasks are split up: the operator only needs to change workpieces and tools, and check for proper operation.

3.   The partially-integrated option applies to a fifth of the cases (19 percent): the operator only tests and corrects the program, the development of which is assigned to a separate programming function.

From these results a pattern of an increasing division of labour is emerging. This is quite in contrast to the Volvo case, which is an example of an increasing integration of tasks. (1)

What are the consequences for the required level of education? In the conventional trajectory, a lower-level technical education is deemed sufficient in ninety percent of all cases. In the computer-controlled trajectory, a lower technical level is deemed adequate in only half of the cases. The required level appears to be related to the level of task integration: in two thirds of the cases to which the integrated option applies an intermediate-level technical education is perceived to be the minimum. However, a lower-level technical education may in some cases be compensated by experience obtained from an apprenticeship. So, employers have some margin to adjust their recruitment behaviour to the state of the labour market (Alders, Christis 1988). Central to this paper is the idea, that the impact of technological change on (regional) labour markets is largely determined by the way employers manage their labour supply. Before we turn to the spatial effects of technological change, some remarks on the goals and instruments of personnel policies are made.

4.   THE ROLE OF PERSONNEL MANAGEMENT

Several instruments can be used by firms in order to procure a sufficient number of employees with the desired qualifications. The main instruments are recruitment, selection and training. The choices made by firms in this respect may have considerable consequences for their relations with the external (regional) labour market. Therefore, the consequences of technological change cannot be assessed without paying attention to the goals and instruments of personnel management.

For firms, both flexibility and stability are important strategic goals. This also holds true with respect to labour. At first sight this seems contradictory. Some authors emphasize the rising importance of flexible labour relations. Others stress the importance of human resource management in order to achieve a stable labour force. Both trends are seen as a response to technological change, but how can they go together?

In firms with an internal labour market, most of the vacancies are filled internally; external recruitment is restricted to a limited number of - mostly low-level jobs. Internal mobility is structured by promotion systems and by internal training facilities. With these measures firms try to achieve a stable labour force. Two conditions for the development of internal labour markets are of special interest in the context of this paper. One is the existence of firm-specific technology and skills. This condition is often supposed to be connected with technological change, because it takes some time before new technologies become standardized. Another condition stimulating internal labour markets is the inability of the labour market to supply employees adequately qualified for the firm's specific needs (Gaspersz, Van Voorden 1987).

How is the goal of flexibility related to the trend towards internal labour markets? Before this question can be answered, some remarks must be made on the various forms of flexibility. First, there is functional and numerical flexibility. By numerical flexibility the amount of labour is varying according to the production volume of the firm: temporary and part-time labour, firing people when sales decrease. Functional flexibility implies that people are supposed to be able to switch tasks, or combine tasks of different levels and disciplines: job rotation, the removal of strict dividing lines between blue and white-collar tasks (like the Volvo case). Secondly, there is internal and external flexibility. Working overtime and internal training are forms of internal flexibility, subcontracting is a form of external flexibility.

Within organizations, different parts often have their own form of flexibility, as Atkinson has made clear (Morris 1988). Therefore, the goals of stability and flexibility do not apply to all parts of the organization to the same extent (Van Ham, Paauwe, Williams 1988). So, stability and flexibility are not as contradictory as it seems. In fact, they are two sides of the same coin. Internal labour markets, for example, require a functionally flexible labour force. The stable positions in some parts of the organization are made possible by the numerical flexibility of other parts.

As a result of technological changes (firm-specific technology and skills) and demographic developments (dejuvenation, greying, rising educational levels) human resources will need more attention. The example of Volvo has illustrated this. Therefore, internal labour markets, in combination with a functionally flexible labour force, will increase in importance.

With the instruments of recruitment, selection, and training, firms try to solve their labour market problems. From the point of view of the demand side, the supply for some jobs may be insufficient, or the qualifications of the labour force are perceived to be inadequate. From the point of view of the supply side, problems may arise concerning the full utilization of the capacities of the employees (Alders, Christis 1988). In the Volvo case we have seen that the problems felt by workers sometimes are an incentive for the development of a new type of personnel management.

To some extent recruitment (external) and training (internal) are interchangeable. Besides, there is some margin to adjust selection criteria to shortages of workers with a certain education. This can be illustrated by the case of the Dutch engineering sector referred to above. For operators of metal-working machines a shift of educational requirements from the lower-technical to the intermediate-technical level has been observed. Nevertheless, only half of the firms (48 percent) requiring an intermediate-level technical education have actually engaged applicants at this level. Why do firms recruit below their standards? Is it because of insufficient labour supply, or because of a deliberate policy? The answer to this question is not the same for all firms and is related to the use of internal recruitment channels.

The actual level of recruitment is connected to the channels used, as can be seen in figure 1. Few firms (10 percent) demanding an intermediate-level technical education limit their search behaviour to external recruitment channels. If they do, they mostly recruit at the intermediate level. Most firms (55 percent), however, limit their recruitment activities to internal channels, in which case the lower-technical level dominates. The two main reasons for recruiting internally are a deliberate internal labour market policy and problems with the supply of labour. The firms combining internal and external recruitment (the remaining 35 percent) do so because of difficulties with the procurement of personnel. In most of these cases applicants at the intermediate-technical level are engaged (Alders, Christis 1988). This example illustrates that firms recruiting internally are less strict about the required formal level of education. Presumably, this is made possible by additional training within the firm.

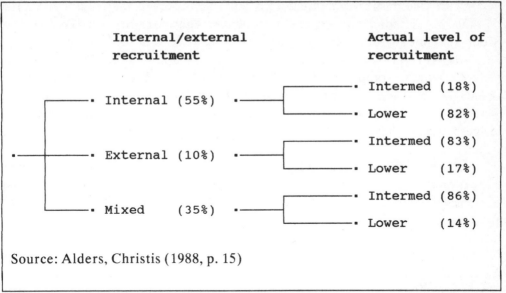

Source: Alders, Christis (1988, p. 15)

Figure 1:   Actual recruitment of machine operators in firms demanding an intermediate-level technical education (share of firms)

The attention given to the training of employees is not isolated from other firm aspects. So far as small and intermediate-sized firms are concerned, it seems that innovative firms stimulate the training of their personnel more than non-innovative firms do. Perhaps innovation and firm-specific skills are related. It is also striking that non-innovative firms express a more negative opinion about the quality of labour supply than their innovative counterparts (Docter 1986). Case studies by the University of Nijmegen reveal the importance attached by successful firms to an internal training policy, both because of its motivating effects on personnel, and because of firm-specific skills which cannot be acquired from the external labour market (Vaessen 1989).

5. SPATIAL OUTCOMES

Technological change, combined with changes in the organization of labour, gives rise to two trends, which might have spatial implications. First, the changing context and methods of production make human skills more central to the strategy of the firm, resulting in higher demands on the level of education of the employees. Related to this is the second trend: the rising importance of internal recruitment and training policies. What do these trends imply for the functioning of regional labour markets?

Before we answer this question it must be observed that regional labour markets in fact consist of different segments. There are two reasons for this. Studies of job search behaviour indicate a positive relationship between the educational level of applicants and the spatial scope of their search process (e.g. Lensink, Vergoossen 1988). The spatial scale of a firm's recruitment behaviour also varies according to the functional level of vacancies (Vos 1980). Therefore, the scale on which the supply and demand of labour are matched ranges from the local to the (inter-)national scale.

As the higher educated are the most mobile part of the labour force, and educational standards of employers are rising, the regional scale seems to become less relevant for the filling of vacancies. This would imply a growing spatial job mobility.

If in the future firms increasingly use internal labour market policies, as an alternative for recruitment on the external market, the effect may be that distance will become even less of a barrier to mobility than it is now. In multi-plant firms at least, distance may to a great extent be overcome by the supply of information on job opportunities at other locations. The internal labour market for top-level functions within the Philips company, for instance, is functioning on a global level.

Partly related to internal labour markets is the increasing use of informal channels, combined with a shift from formal to informal selection criteria. According to Windolf, Wood (1988) 'extended internal labour markets' are becoming increasingly important. As social networks (e.g. friends and relatives of employees) tend to be spatially biased, one would expect contraction of the firm's recruitment areas. The expected spatial outcomes of both trends are therefore contradictory.

6. CONCLUSION

In this paper, we have demonstrated some of the effects of technological changes in manufacturing on qualitative labour demand. Technological changes, however, are strongly related to changes in the environment of the firm (markets, competition) and their effects on labour to a large extent are co-determined by the internal organization and strategy of the firm. In this respect we have given special attention to the way firms manage their personnel supply by means of their recruitment and training policy.

Technological change, therefore, is only one of the factors affecting labour demand. Nevertheless, profound changes can be expected. Whether increasing integration or division of tasks will occur, largely depends on the choices firms make with respect to their labour organization and personnel policy. As for the spatial outcomes of these technological and organizational changes, the direction of change is not very clear. One reason for this might be that a gap exists between theories on firm behaviour on one hand and theories on spatial labour market processes on the other hand.

NOTES

1   The automobile industry and the engineering industry, however, have highly divergent starting points. Until recently, the engineering industry has not been very liable to a sharp division of labour typical of Taylorism, because of its short series. The automobile industry, in contrast, has always been an example of mass production based on assembly lines. Moreover, one should be aware that Volvo is known for its reputation as far as its personnel management is concerned. Though Volvo may be somewhat atypical for the current practice, it may be an indicator of changes to be expected in the near future.

REFERENCES

Alders, B., J. Christis (1988), *Technologie, organisatie en arbeidsmarkt. Een onderzoek naar de functieveranderingen en recruteringsstrategieën in de Nederlandse industrie.* Paper voor het Symposium Technologie - Economie, 31 maart 1988, 's-Gravenhage.

Alvstam, C.G., K. Ellegard (forthcoming), *Volvo. The organization of work: a determinant of the future location of manufacturing enterprises.* In: M. de Smidt, E. Wever (forthcoming), The corporate firm in a changing world economy: case studies in the geography of enterprise. Routledge, London.

Bekkering, J.M., J.S. Cramer, I.A.M. Oud (1988), *Technologische ontwikkeling en de opleiding van de werkzame beroepsbevolking. Een bedrijfstakkenanalyse.* Paper voor het Symposium Technologie - Economie, 31 maart 1988, 's-Gravenhage.

Cooke, P. (1988), *Flexible integration, scope economies, and strategic alliances: social and spatial mediations. Environment and Planning D,* Society & Space, nr. 3, p. 281 - 300.

Docter, H.J. (1986), *Innovatiebevordering*. Economisch-Statistische Berichten, 17-9, p. 904 - 909.

Fruytier, B. (1989), *Taylorisme of het nieuwe produktiekoncept? De economische effecten van de invoering van CNC-machines*. Tijdschrift voor Politieke Economie, nr. 1, p. 79-103.

Fuchs, M., E.W. Schamp (1989), *Standard Elektrik Lorenz. Introducing CAD into a telecommunications firm: its impact on labour*. In: M. de Smidt, E. Wever (forthcoming), The corporate firm in a changing world economy: case studies in the geography of enterprise. Routledge, London.

Gaspersz, J.B.R., W. van Voorden (1987), *Spatial aspects of internal labour markets*. Tijdschrift voor Economische en Sociale Geografie, nr. 5, p. 359 - 365.

Ham, J.C. van, J. Paauwe, A.R.T. Williams (1988), *Human resource management en transactiekostenbenadering*. Economisch-Statistische Berichten, 23-11, p. 1109 - 1112.

Kaplinsky, R. (1987), *Micro-electronics and employment revisited: a review*. International Labour Office, Geneva.

Lensink, E., T. Vergoossen (1988), *Wervingsgedrag van bedrijven en arbeidsmarktoriëntatie van werkzoekenden in Noordoost-Brabant*. Geografisch en Planologisch Instituut, KU Nijmegen / Gewestelijk Arbeidsbureau Oss-Cuyk / Gewestelijk Arbeidsbureau Veghel/Uden.

Morris, J.L. (1988), *New technologies, flexible work practices, and regional sociospatial differentiation: some observations from the United Kingdom*. Environment and Planning D, Society & Space, nr. 3, p. 301 - 319.

Schoenberger, E. (1988), *From Fordism to flexible accumulation: technology, competitive strategies, and international location*. Environment and Planning D, Society & Space, nr. 3, p. 245 - 262.

Scott, A.J., P. Cooke (1988), *The new geography and sociology of production*. Environment and Planning D, Society & Space, nr. 3, p. 241 - 244.

Vaessen, P. (1989), *Bedrijf, regio en succes; een micro-onderzoek.* Vakgroep Sociale en Economische Geografie, Faculteit der Beleidswetenschappen, KU Nijmegen.

Veld, J. in 't (1981), *Organisatiestructuur en arbeidsplaats. De organisatie van mensen en middelen: theorie en praktijk.* Elsevier, Amsterdam/Brussel.

Vos, J.H. (1980), *Mobiliteitsbereidheid op de arbeidsmarkt.* Economisch-Statistische Berichten, 30-4, p. 519 - 522.

Windolf, P., S. Wood (1988), *Recruitment and selection in the labour market. A comparative study of Britain and West Germany.* Avebury, Aldershot.

NEW CONCEPTS OF MEASURING TECHNOLOGICAL CHANGE

Knut Koschatzky
Fraunhofer-Institute for Systems and Innovation Research
(FhG-ISI), Karlsruhe

1.   INTRODUCTION

It has becoming increasingly important with regard to the growing international competition in industry in the fields of industrial innovation as well as research to have available rational methods of determining the state of the art of technology on an international comparative basis.

Especially in the late 70s and early 80s the fear of an increasing technological gap between Western Europe and the USA on one hand and Japan on the other revived. Parallel to the introduction of technological "anti-gap" policies of certain countries, projects and studies were embarked upon, or resumed, concerning the question of a quantitative measuring of technical standards and shortfalls. Relevant work came from Japan, North America and Western Europe.

The results of research and development (R&D) as well as the market success of technically new products cannot be measured in terms of the customary scientific understanding of "measuring" a variable. A way out of these difficulties is the use of **indicators**. Indicators must be viewed as "representatives" for the actual variables and are not identical to R&D or innovation output or success. Major effectiveness can therefore only be achieved through qualitative interpretation and the synopsis of the largest possible number of different kind of indicators for studying innovation dynamics and the technological change.

A systematic distinction can be made in line with the chronological sequence of innovation processes between expenditure, throughput and returns (or output) indicators.

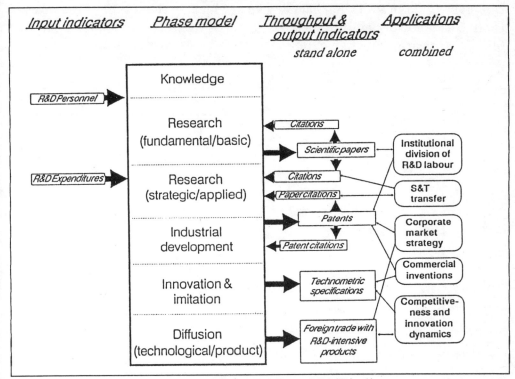

FIGURE 1:   Input-Output Model for R&D and S&T indicators

The figure maps the various types of science and technology (S&T) indicators being used in R&D and innovation studies in respect to six stages which are commonly differentiated for the sake of analytical clarity. In reality, of course, the borderlines between these stages are unclear as the innovation process is not linear.

Most popular, since the figures are easily obtainable, is the description of innovation processes and the quantity of sectorial or national R&D by using the **input-indicators "R&D personnel"** and **"R&D expenditures"**. Often used in respect to international comparisons is the R&D intensity (gross R&D expenditure per gross domestic product).

Figure 2 illustrates the R&D performance of OECD countries in 1985 in relation to their foreign trade specialization in R&D-intensive products 1986 (the RCA indicator will be explained later on). As expected, Japan, the USA, Sweden, and West Germany are in the lead, whereas in Portugal, Greece and Turkey R&D only plays a minor role. Nevertheless, it has to be emphasized that the input-indicators only allow interpretation on the amount of manpower and capital invested in R&D, but cannot give any idea on the results of the invested capital, as not every million spent on research yields to corresponding results. Still, for the early detection of innovation processes, personnel and expenditure figures are a useful tool.

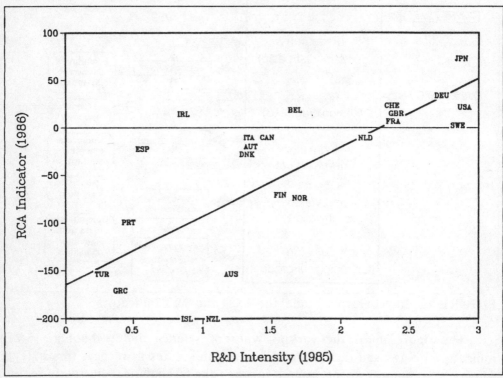

FIGURE 2: R&D intensity and foreign trade specialization in OECD countries 1985

The results of **fundamental or basic research** cannot be described or analysed with economic figures, as neither figures can be obtained nor are the results of basic research patentable. For example, the direct success of space, defense and health research are not reflected in the national productivity accounts, as Griliches (1987) mentioned. For that case the only possible indicators used in recent studies are article counts in scientific journals and citation analysis.

Patents can be used for the measurement of development output, sometimes years ahead of the market introduction of a new product or process. In general, there are two faces of patent indicators: on one hand the development success is documented; on the other, economic interest in certain future markets is indicated, especially by applying for a foreign patent. Therefore, a good patent indicator for the measurement of development output is not automatically good for the measurement of potential innovations (market success). Depending on the problem, selective use of various indicators should be made. This is not only true for patents, but for the whole indicator system.

Foreign trade statistics are also included in the indicator system, for example to "measure" trade in R&D-intensive products. Despite the fact that there are different lists in use for defining R&D-intensive products, foreign trade figures can easily be found. The problem with this indicator is that

- the breakdown of the product groups is not as deep as to effectively analyse specific products
- trade figures only show the market results of innovations but not the creation of the innovation which is usually some years ahead of market introduction and product trading.

Also the causes of success or failure in the innovation process remain open. Posner (1961) mentioned that trade may be caused by the existence of some technical know-how in one country not available elsewhere, even though there may be no international differences in relative endowment of factors of production. This is why trade figures can supplement analysis on innovation dynamics, but should not be used as the methodical basis for such analysis because of the time lag inherent in trade figures.

A new concept in the field of so-called output indicators has been developed since the end of 1984 as part of the activities pursued by our institute. This method, called **technometrics**, permits systematic international comparison between specifications covering new products or processes already on the market or still in the laboratory stage.

The technometric indicators are established in a direct relation to the trade-figures as well as to patent and literature statistics. Thus, it is possible to detect lines of research and innovation dynamics from the early stages and to convert them into an output-oriented description of the efficiency of science and technology activities. As reported before, the various S&T indicators should be used only selective, depending on the type of R&D to be studied.

One should also bear in mind that the indicators are the tool of analysis, not its results. Only combining indicator figures is not sufficient to assess the process of R&D and innovation. A proper interpretation of the findings based on expert opinion has to be given. As the technometric method draws on expert knowledge, this particular indicator may play a central role in an indicator network.

Therefore, this paper concentrates on the technometrics approach as a new concept of measuring technological change.

2. TECHNOMETRIC MODEL

The term "technometrics" is ambiguous: for one thing it was formed in analogy with "econometrics" and "bibliometrics" and means the "measurement of technology"; for another, it designates a specific metrication in the mathematical sense.

Technometrics aims at the determination of technical specifications of national products and processes and their international comparison. This means that the basis of this concept is not formed by whole branches or product groups, but by the different technical specifications of a single product or process.

Technometric indicators are aggregated numbers composed of several technical specifications of a technique or product, i.e. of various physical units. So, the individual element of the indicator is the technical characteristic.

Characteristics define either a property of the product or the production process. If the same product or process is capable of serving different purposes simultaneously, for which the characteristics vary in their importance, functional characteristics or weighted priorities have to be introduced. Whereas process and product characteristics contain discrete physical entities and are hence objective, the functional characteristics, or priority lists, contain individual or collective considerations concerning the purposes of the product or the process and cannot, therefore, be objective.

One of the first tasks within the approach is the selection of product specifications. It is done in a kind of delphi-study by asking experts from industry and research (in Fraunhofer-Society we have the advantage of easy access to experts in different fields of technology) for important specifications of the products or processes to be investigated. The derived specification lists will then be discussed, adjusted and sometimes reduced and constitute the basis for data collection. For both reasons, building specification lists and collecting data, technometrics relies heavily on experts' opinion.

Contrary to the use of economic figures and indicators, the approach cannot utilize data already computed in several statistics, but has to produce its own data. These data are derived from technical data sheets and exhibition literature, and above all, as a result of a large number of personal discussions and interviews with experts in industrial development laboratories on the basis of a pre-prepared specification questionnaire.

Technological disparities within an economy are excluded from the investigation, since different national firms competing with one another can all profit from the same R&D know-how, the same human capital and the same research infrastructure. Therefore, the highest technical standards among domestic firms are in each case regarded as the national standard. For that reason the technologically leading company in the special field to be investigated has to be found. If it is included, and it usually is by asking experts or by asking companies for their strongest competitor, the representative character of the results is always ensured. By scanning the industrial landscape a lot of additional information on a micro-level can be derived. But they do not show up on a company basis in any written report. These information are only used for a better assessment of the calculated technometric figures since technometrics is based on a confidential relation between industry and our institute.

Approximately ten thousand technical specifications covering products and processes from West Germany, the United States, Japan, and other countries have been stored in the institute's computer-aided technometric cadastre since 1986. Fields under investigation have been:

- Enzymes (immobilized biocatalysts)
- Genetically engineered medical drugs
- Solar cells and modules
- Laser beam sources
- Sensors
- Industrial robots
- Medical diagnostics (DNA-probe-diagnostics and monoclonal antibodies)
- Biological waste-water treatment.

The problem with single technological specifications is that they may be ranked, but cannot be cardinally aggregated to form indicators. A metric system, therefore, must be introduced. It consists of a transformation of the technical characteristics into a dimensionless intervall [0,1]. If countries are compared by technological specifications one by one (no aggregation), then the metric conserves the ordinal ranking of the original figures. In aggregate technometric indicators those items with considerable international disparities dominate the distinctions and indicator values.

$$K*(i,j,k)= \frac{K_{max} (i,j,k) - K_{min} (i,j,k_{min})}{K_{max} (i,j,k_{max}) - K_{min} (i,j,k_{min})}$$

K * = Metric specification figure
i   = product or process
j   = technical specification
k   = subset (company, group of institutions, country) index

K_{max} (i,j,k) is the maximum value of the specification j of product i under investigation in subset k
K_{min} (i,j,k_{min}) is the minimum value of the specification recorded in all investigated subsets
K_{max} (i,j,k_{max}) is the maximum value of the specification recorded for all subsets.

FIGURE 3:   Technometric metric

The formula can be explained as follows:

The technological standard of the country which has made the greatest progress in terms of the specifications under review defines the international maximum value K * = 1. The metric value for the other countries is determined by the spread of the standards within each country and between different countries.

If the scale of the specification is inverse, e.g. in fuel consumption of cars, that is, if the minimum value of K represents the highest technological level, an inverse formula holds.

The different K values of specifications which describe one product or process, are then aggregated into a product or process K-value; in case of equal important specifications just by calculating the average, in the other case by weighing each specification and calculating the weighted average. Different K-values of products and processes in one technological field can also be combined into one overall indicator, but with the result of hiding product or specification information.

In literature, a number of similar approaches can be found, but only very few of the proposed concepts aim at a quantitative comparison of purely technological specifications at an international level.

Introducing the three categories:

- contemporary analysis
- technological analysis and
- international comparable analysis,

out of the few publications which fulfill all three conditions, two are from Manchester University.

Gibbons, Coombs, Saviotti and Stubbs (1982) presented pure technological data on tractors in the UK market. UK firms, West German, Italian and COMECON companies are compared between 1957 and 1977. The same is done for tractors present on the Dutch market.

Saviotti (1985) additionally supplies evidence on motor car technology on the UK market from 1955 to 1983. Priorities or weighting of the technical specifications are determined either by factor analysis or by a hedonic price method.

Thus, the technometric method seems to fill an analytical gap in the framework of S&T indicators.

Compared to all S&T indicators in use (as shown in FIGURE 1), the technometric method is less well-established. Most of the authors in innovation research regard the intermingling of technical information and data with economic information as useless. But the distinction between specification data and economics does not mean that international trade figures and suchlike can be neglected. On the contrary, it is suggested and also done in our studies, to supplement technical indicators by exactly or fairly exactly corresponding trade figures without mixing the data. Keeping economic and technometric indicators apart from each other makes it possible to find "additional clues". Experts may be confronted with (contradictory) technological and econometric figures of the same technology and may find explanations only through these "eye-opening" indicators. In other words, new technologies are hard to define and analyse without explicit incorporation of the knowledge of the science and engineering communities.

3. EXAMPLE - MONOCLONAL ANTIBODIES

Antibodies are produced by the B-cells of the immune system. Formerly, they were produced by immunizing test animals with antigens. The extracted antisera contained different antibodies, which all could be directed against the same antigen, but were different in their characteristics (polyclonal antibodies).

In 1975, Milstein and Koehler published their pioneering studies on the in-vitro synthesis of monoclonal antibodies for which they were awarded the Nobel Prize in medicine in 1984.

These monoclonal antibodies are used for immuno-assays. The most important applications in immuno-diagnostics can be found in the fields of thyroid diagnostics, sexual hormons, tumor markers, infectional diseases and the control of blood banks, for example on HTLV-1, Syphillis, Hepatitis B, HIV.

Immuno-diagnostics on the basis of monoclonal antibodies play an important role in modern biotechnology. The annual world market for immuno-diagnostics and immuno-asssay-kits is estimated at more than 5 billion US $, out of which 40% are generated in the USA, 10% in Japan and approximately 10% in Western Europe.

Immuno-diagnostics on the basis of monoclonal antibodies had been a major subject in a recently completed technometrics project, financed by the Ministry of Research and Technology (BMFT) in Bonn. Project manager was Dr. Reiss of the department of Technological Change in FhG-ISI. Some of his findings will be used for a short demonstration of the technometric approach.

Figure 4 shows the technometric profile of four different tests in thyroid diagnostics for Germany (DE), the US and Japan as of 1989. The tests are:

T3:   Triiodothyronine
T4:   Thyroxin
FT4:   Free Thyroxin
TSH: Thyroid-stimulating hormone

Each of the tests is characterised by 5 resp. 6 different specifications:

- Sensitivity
- Intra-assay precision
- Inter-assay precision

- Measurement range
- Test duration
- Handling

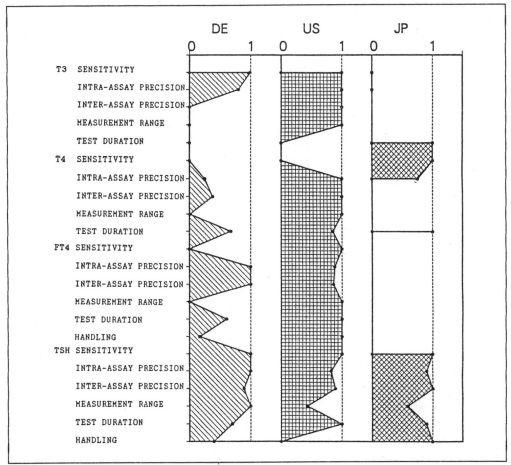

FIGURE 4   Technometric profile of selected immuno-assays in thyroid diagnostics in 1989

In most cases the US reached an indicator value of 1 which means that the "best" product specification can be found among US manufacturers. In some cases also Germany and Japan reached highest specifications. A "0" does not mean worst technology, but well introduced on the market with no heights or downs. It marks the lowest (in inverse cases the highest) specification value out of the (representative) sample.

At this point it has to be repeated that the technometric indicator should not be interpreted in a way of economic competitiveness. A highest specification value only indicates that in the specific field of technology a country offers the best technical performance. It may not mean that the product is already successfully marketed and that it is the leading product in its field. It may be excellent but not worth its price or, there is not yet an application sophisticated enough.

As a next step the specification values can be combined in an aggregated technometric indicator for each test. This has been done in figure 5.

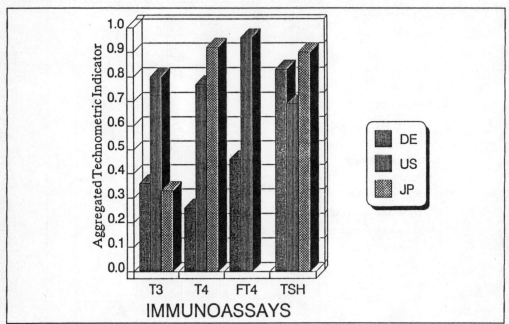

FIGURE 5: Aggregated technometric indicator of selected immuno-assays as of 1989

For the 4 tests in our example West Germany's international position does not rank highest, but shows a second rank in TSH. In other tests either the US or Japan are in the lead. For FT4, there were no data from Japan obtainable.

In a third step also the combination of the technometric figures of the different tests in one aggregate technometric indicator for the whole technological field is possible. At this point, we hide a lot of the specific information the approach is able to generate, but political and governmental decision makers always require broad figures which give an impression of the overall technological position of a country.

For the whole antibody diagnostica investigated the technometric indicator shows the leading technological position of the US, followed by West Germany and Japan. A detailed interpretation, which can be found in the final project report, shows that the technical standard of more traditional products between Germany, the USA and Japan is fairly equal. But great differences can be observed in new developments, especially in the field of genetic engineering, where the US rank first. Japan is quite strong in test automation, whereas West Germany shows good performance in the tests already introduced on the market.

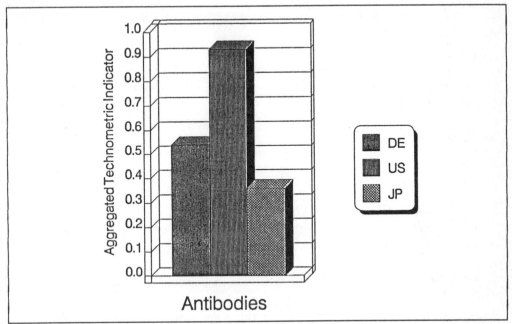

FIGURE 6:   Technometric indicators for monoclonal antibodies as of 1989

As mentioned before, the whole approach does not consist of calculating technometric indicators only, but also includes economic indicators, especially trade figures and patent statistics.

The question arises if there is indeed the need to conduct costly and time consuming studies for technical monitoring, or if there are other, more established indicators which can be used for the same purpose.

In other studies analysing the international competitiveness of West Germany, we use, for example, data from the international and national trade statistics.

Besides the problem that the trade classification is mostly somewhat broader than the specific technologies to be investigated, the most important objection is that it is only possible to analyse products (not so much processes) which are already on the market. For monitoring new technologies still in the laboratory or testing stage, trade figures are an inefficient tool.

For illustrating in the project the international position of the FRG on diagnostics, data from the German trade statistics were used. The breakdown of goods is according to the "Warenverzeichnis für die Außenhandelsstatistik 1987".

The problem with immuno-assays on the basis of monoclonal antibodies is that they are mingled in two groups:

- Group No. 3002 110: "Sera of immunized animals or humans"
- Group No. 3819 620: "Laboratory reactive means without those to analyse blood groups or blood factors".

To gain a better insight into the figures, special coefficients were calculated. These are:

1. The Standard Price (price per weight) [V/kg]
2. The Export/Import Ratio [E/I]
3. The Supply Share of different countries to the German market [Supp.Sh.]
4. The Revealed Comparative Advantage [RCA].

The RCA indicates the extent to which export surpluses in the product groups under consideration deviate altogether from the average for manufactured industrial products. In the logarithmic version positive values indicate an above-average position and comparative advantages in the product group. The formula is shown in the following figure.

$$RCA_{ij} = 100 \left\{ \ln \left(\frac{E_{ij}}{I_{ij}} : \frac{R_j \; E_{ij}}{R_j \; I_{ij}} \right) \right\}$$

E = Exports   i = Country
I = Imports   j = Product

FIGURE 7: RCA formula

The RCA analyses the bilateral trade relations. Not considering the overall world trade has its reason in the fact that the advanced economies do not always supply products of the same technological content to the various regions of the world, for example appropriate technologies to the developing countries. Therefore, to avoid inhomogenities, the bilateral trade relations between the most advanced economies are preferable. But the analysis is then biased towards "one country under review".

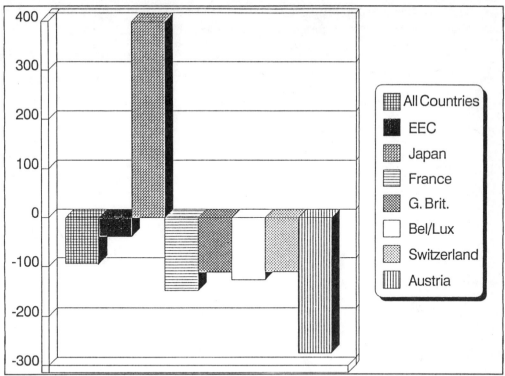

FIGURE 8   Foreign trade indicator RCA 1987

In our example the focus will be on the sera. The only country under review is the FRG. The figures show that the position of West Germany is quite weak. In 1987 the RCA for West Germany's trade with the EEC countries was - 39, with France and Great Britain much less. Only in the trade relations with Japan West Germany gained comparative advantages - at a Japanese supply share of 0.3%.

No RCA-value could be calculated for the US, as there were no German exports of sera to the US in 1987.

Using these results alone, it will not be possible to derive a clear picture of Germany's international technological position in immuno-diagnostics. Not only are trade figures too late, but also is the breakdown much too unspecific to supply detailed information on this technological field. But in other cases, either when the technology is clearly represented in trade statistics or when the search-strategy is open and the analysis does not start from one very specific technology, then trade figures are indeed able to produce an overview over the international competitiveness in, say, leading-edge technologies, respectively products comprising such technologies which are already on the market. But the task was, frankly speaking, to present some impressions on the highlights of the technometric approach on a very disaggregated level.

Foreign Trade Figures 1987
Fed. Rep. of Germany
Sera of Immunized Animals or Humans

COUNTRY	UNIT	1987
All Countries	V/kg	359
	E/I	0.58
	RCA	-94
EEC	V/kg	194
	E/I	0.97
	Supp.Sh. (%)	23.51
	RCA	-39
France	V/kg	381
	E/I	0.33
	Supp.Sh.(%)	2.60
	RCA	-148
USA	V/kg	230
	E/I	E=0
	Supp.Sh.(%)	16.94
	RCA	--

TABLE 1   Other foreign trade indicators 1987

4. SUMMARY

The technometric concept is a technic-oriented approach which aims at using technical specifications for contemporary international comparisons of technological positions. It provides important information which cannot be read directly from market results alone. This paper concentrated on technometrics, but there are also other methods to be used, like bibliometrics, patent statistics and trade figures.

It should be clear that the technometric approach, besides its major advantages, is also subject to some restrictions. These include:

- the need to produce own data which is time-consuming and cost-intensive;

- the fact that no open search-strategy will be possible so that only technical segments and not the whole range of R&D activities can be analysed;

- the fact that the technometric examination contains no standardisation for the size of a country, its R&D budget or its R&D personnel;

- up till now only experiences in highly developed countries with a wide range of companies have been made. It has still to be proved if technometrics is also an instrument for evaluating the technical performance of smaller countries or newly industrialising countries with only a limited range of nationally technical leading companies which would perhaps not supply sufficient information. A joint project on this topic has just recently started in cooperation with the Neaman Institute of the Technion in Israel.

Because of these restrictions and unsolved questions, it is suggested to strengthen the network of output indicators by creating correspondences between the classification systems. In the example presented in this paper, the breakdown of the trade statistics was much too broad to cope with immuno diagnostics. When introducing patent analysis, concordance problems of combining the Standard International Trade Classification with the International Patent Classification and, may be also, with the Standard Industrial Classification will arise.

If various comparative indicators are combined and the concordance problem will be solved, then an evaluative type of assessment seems to be possible. For evaluation purposes, integrated networks of data have to be constructed, causal or statistical relationships have to be verified. But it should not be assumed that the various indicator relationships always result in highly significant positive correlations. The input-output-model (Fig. 1) suggests that the indicators are not equally valid for a study of the various R&D and innovation phases and the various R&D-performing groups of institutions. As results from studies made in our institute show, that in many cases, however, with allowance for time lags between the indicators, a highly significant positive correlation may be found. For example, in leading-edge technologies patent indicators are approximately two to three years "earlier" than marketable results, i.e. trade indicators (Schmoch 1988, 21). Still, most sets of indicators are far from being complete. Therefore, peer evaluation and personal expertise are an essential addition to science and technology indicators to bridge the inconsistencies and the lack of adaptation within the indicator system. As the technometric approach is largely based on expert interviews, the technometric indicator plays a central role in any science and technology indicator network and in the measurement of technological change.

NOTE

This paper is based on the findings of a team of researchers in the department of Technological Change of the Fraunhofer-Institute for Systems and Innovation Research, led by the head of department, Dr. H. Grupp.

The author thanks for drawing on publications from H. Grupp and Th. Reiss and also for their friendly cooperation.

REFERENCES

M. Gibbons, R. Coombs, P. Saviotti and P.C. Stubbs, *Innovation and Technical Change,* Research Policy 11 (1982) 289-310.

Z. Griliches, *R&D and Productivity: Measurement Issues and Econometric Results,* Science 237 (1987) 31-35.

H. Grupp, *The measurement of technical performance in the framework of R&D intensity, patent, and trade indicators,* paper submitted to Research Policy (1990).

H. Grupp, O. Hohmeyer, *Technological Standards for Research-Intensive Product Groups,* in: A.F.J. van Raan (ed.), Handbook of Quantitative Studies of Science and Technology (Elsevier, Amsterdam, 1988).

H. Grupp, O. Hohmeyer, R. Kollert, H. Legler, *Technometrie - Die Bemessung des technisch-wirtschaftlichen Leistungsstands* (TÜV Rheinland, Cologne, 1987).

M.V. Posner, *Technical Change and International Trade,* Oxford Economic Papers 13 (1961) 323.341.

T. Reiss, O. Hohmeyer, H. Grupp, *Bemessung des technisch-wirtschaftlichen Leistungsstandes der Bundesrepublik Deutschland, der Vereinigten Staaten und Japans in Teilbereichen der Biotechnologie (Technometrie II),* Forschungsbericht PLI 13743 an den BMFT (Karlsruhe, 1989).

P.P. Saviotti, *An Approach to the Measurement of Technology Based on the Hedonic Price Method and Related Methods,* Tech. Forecast. Soc. Change 27 (1985) 309-334.

U. Schmoch, H. Grupp, W. Mannsbart, B. Schwitalla, *Technikprognosen mit Patentindikatoren* (TÜV Rheinland, Cologne, 1988).

ADDRESSES

Prof. Dr. Ulrich C.H. Blum
Otto-Friedrich-Universität
Volkswirtschaftslehre,
insb. Wirtschaftspolitik
Feldkirchenstraße 21
D-8500 Bamberg
F.R. of Germany

Prof. Dr. Friedrich Buttler
Institut für Arbeitsmarkt- und Berufsforschung
der Bundesanstalt für Arbeit
Postfach
D-8500 Nürnberg
F.R. of Germany

Prof. Dr. D.J. van de Kaa
Netherlands Institute for Advanced Study in
the Humanities and Social Sciences
Meijboomlaan 1
2242 PR Wassenaar
Netherlands

Dr. K. Koschatzky
Fraunhofer-Institut ISI
Breslauer Straße 48
D-7500 Karlsruhe 1
F.R. of Germany

Prof. Dr. Robert M. Lindley
Institute for Employment Research
University of Warwick
Coventry, CV4 7AL
Great Britain

Dr. Ulrich Mammey
Deutsches Institut für Bevölkerungswissenschaften
Postfach 5528
6200 Wiesbaden
F.R. of Germany

Prof. Dr. Josef Schmid
Otto-Friedrich-Universität
Lehrstuhl für Bevölkerungswissenschaft
Hornthalstraße 2
D-8500 Bamberg
F.R. of Germany

Prof. Dr. G. Tziafetas
Greek Productivity Centre
28 Kapodistriou Str.
Athens 106 82
Greece

Drs. Sake Wagenaar
Prof. Dr. Egbert Wever
Department of Economic Geography
University of Nijmegen
P.O.Box 9044
6500 KD Nijmegen
Netherlands